HOW TO LIVE
FOREVER

HOW TO LIVE
FOREVER

A Guide to Writing
the Final Chapter of
Your Life Story

KIMBERLY BEST

WESTBOW
PRESS®
A DIVISION OF THOMAS NELSON
& ZONDERVAN

WestBow Press books may be ordered through booksellers or by contacting:

WestBow Press
A Division of Thomas Nelson & Zondervan
1663 Liberty Drive
Bloomington, IN 47403
www.westbowpress.com
1 (866) 928-1240

ISBN: 978-1-9736-7533-4 (sc)
ISBN: 978-1-9736-7534-1 (hc)
ISBN: 978-1-9736-7532-7 (e)

Library of Congress Control Number: 2019914848

Print information available on the last page.

WestBow Press rev. date: 10/11/2019

Dedication

This book is dedicated in honor of my ancestors - my roots, whose stories I hardly know. I am me because of you. I can't imagine the courage of your journey.

And for my descendants - my children and my grandchildren, the bright, new growth on the family tree. In you, I see the gift of legacy.
I couldn't love you more.

Contents

The Most Meaningful Things

For some people, mostly elite soldiers, police, first responders, or race car drivers going 200 miles per hour into a turn, there is a very real awareness that this could be one's last day. But for most of us, we push away and ignore any thoughts of our own death. Yet, the most meaningful things are often the ones we pay the least attention to. This is particularly true with the last chapter of the stories of our lives.

In reality, most of us do have the chance during those years or months that make up the closing chapters of our lives to make a difference. That is, *if we took the time* and *if we knew how and what to do* in order to close loops, prepare our lives, and provide well for our loved ones, then we could make those precious final days that much more meaningful. Even simply capturing the priceless stories that live within us can indeed help us live forever in the hearts and minds of our family and friends.

But none of that happens by accident. If we're honest, we know that we're experts at ignoring and pushing off any thoughts of death. Unless death has been forced upon us, like in losing a parent or a loved one in an accident, we often have no idea how many important (and too-often ignored) decisions, omissions, and actions can make someone's ending either a blessing or an incredible burden.

And I don't think it's an accident you picked up this book. Because unlike any book I've read, Kim Best uses her skills as a nurse and as a professional mediator to lay before us a road less traveled. This thoughtfully guides the reader down a path that combines Kim's compassion, servanthood, and how-to knowledge to prepare well on the nursing side with the wisdom, calm, and insight to deal with the messy conflicts and difficult situations that aging and death can cause.

Kim steps right into this fearful, untrodden place. Her stories will grab your heart and motivate you to do more with the last chapter of your life than you ever thought about before. This book will offer you more ways to get centered, more clarity on how to gather the specifics you'll need to be prepared, and more wisdom on how to keep your loved ones from spending countless hours reconstructing your wishes or having to endure legal and personal trials. At the same time, you will gain clarity around how to walk through your end of life with courage and compassion, and you will learn ways to capture the stories of your life that can guide and inspire generations far beyond your last day.

If you have ever traveled overseas to someplace new, you know it's nice to have a map. But it's an incredible gift to have a world-class guide show up, right when you need her. You need this book, and Kim Best, I believe, is that world-class guide you need when it comes to end-of-life issues. She is that person who can guide you to finishing well. Such a fearful, difficult time can hold so much promise and faith and love and life. As a guide, Kim can take you to the places that bring hope and inspire love and generosity, and she can steer you away from the things that have absolutely ruined too many lives at the very end.

In short, you want to finish well. You want to write that final chapter in a way that gives inspiration to others, and to not just fade out or flame out and burn others. From family dynamics to crucial health decisions, must-do legal details, and getting comfortable with this uncomfortable area, you've picked the right guide. Now you just have to act and follow the path that Kim leads you down.

I don't like to think about it or admit it, but I'm in that last chapter of life, and so is my wife, Cindy. So, we're not only clicking the box as friends of Kim Best, but we are working through her book together because we want to better love each other and have our last chapter bless our children and now grandchildren. What Kim Best lays out is a process. It's a wonderful guide to gather memories and have those needed conversations to, in Kim's words, "Leave your legacy with purpose."

John Trent, PhD
President, StrongFamilies.com
Author of _The Blessing_ and _Life Mapping_

This is the true joy in life, the being used for a purpose recognized by yourself as a mighty one; the being thoroughly worn out before you are thrown on the scrap heap; the being a force of Nature instead of a feverish selfish little clod of ailments and grievances complaining that the world will not devote itself to making you happy. I am of the opinion that my life belongs to the community, and as long as I live, it is my privilege to do for it whatever I can. I want to be thoroughly used up when I die, for the harder I work, the more I live. Life is no "brief candle" to me. It is a sort of splendid torch which I have got hold of for a moment, and I want to make it burn as brightly as possible before handing it on to the future generations.
—GEORGE BERNARD SHAW

Introduction: It's Your Story

For human beings, life is meaningful
because it is a story, and in
stories, endings matter.
—ATUL GAWANDE, *BEING MORTAL*

I will never forget the first patient I saw die. She was old and ill and beyond the curatives of modern medicine. I sat beside her bedside because I believed strongly that dying was something that should be shared. I believed then, and still do, that no one should die alone. I felt that this woman's life was a story, and she should not be alone in her final chapter.

Even as a young woman early in my nursing career, I was awed by the beauty of dying. It was a messy, sad, fragile, beautiful event. In this way, I was struck by how closely dying resembled birth, which is also poignantly beautiful and messy. These two life events are different sides of the same coin, and both are awe-inspiring, sacred moments. Yet, even at these early stages of reflection, I understood that for some reason our society celebrates birth but shies away from the topic of dying. To me, this seemed inherently wrong and backward. Why do we glorify the start of life but deeply fear its end?

Witnessing death was beautiful to me because, although I didn't really know this person except as my patient that day, I knew that she had a story. I wondered what that story was. I sat beside her, and I wondered what she was like as a little girl. I wondered if her dreams had come true, what her disappointments were, and how she forged on through both triumphs and losses. I wondered whom she loved and who loved her, what she was proud of, and what she regretted. I wished that she could tell me her story. I wished for her that she left with someone truly knowing her.

As I sat with this woman during her last moments of life, I looked at her, and I was struck by the realization that life is like a book. We open the first chapter with our birth, and then the story grows. Our lives advance and so does the character list of meaningful people who surround us. We overcome obstacles like a literary hero and experience devastating losses like a Shakespearean tragedy. Despite the ups and downs and, for many, the lack of a tidy narrative arc, our lives progress and expand into beautiful, utterly unique stories. Our stories. In these story that are solely our own, our dying is the last chapter of our books. The end.

For the woman in the hospital bed in front of me, her story was at its end. As her personal book began to close, she was taking most of her chapters with her—countless stories that go unshared, maybe even including the essence of who she really was. She lived, she conquered, she touched people, she loved, she hated, she worked, she played, she likely raised children, she impacted other lives, and she died. The beginning of life is a celebration. Maybe, the end should be as well.

Now, I don't even know the number of people I have sat beside as they died. My career as an intensive care nurse and then an emergency room nurse gave me witness to many people dying in many different circumstances at many different ages. From the womb to the elderly, I have felt privileged to be present as many people closed the back covers of their individual stories.

In addition to the privilege of spending time with people and their families in the terminal moments of their lives, I also have had the privilege of facilitating discussions on many final-chapter conversations. Following my career in nursing, I chose to start a new chapter of my own life and cultivate my passion about communication, especially when communication is most difficult. To pursue this passion, I studied psychology and conflict management. In the many roles that I have played thus far in my life—nurse, mediator, conflict manager, friend, sister, daughter, and mother—I have participated in countless conversations around choices and decisions that were last chapter.

I love my job as a mediator. I get to help people who are stuck in conflict. I help them take down the walls and build bridges. I help them hear and understand each other and be heard and understood. I help them learn how to communicate more effectively. Mediation is an amazing tool for helping opposing sides, views, and desires come together and reach an agreement that satisfies both sides, and it is a wonderful alternative to litigation. When we are so angry that we take someone to court, the expenses are huge. Anger, fear, and resentment grow. Usually one person loses and one person wins, and the fate of that is left up to a judge. In mediation, people get to come into an agreement that is mutually beneficial. Problems are solved collaboratively, and everyone has a voice. There is no need to make up a story about the other's motives, feelings, or intentions. We can talk about them. Rather than have the separateness and acrimony of a lawsuit, relationships can almost always be salvaged, if not enhanced. Resolving conflict in a win-win enhances relationships, and this is especially important at the end of life.

One of my mediation clients, a ninety-year-old, very successful attorney now preparing for his last chapter, had all of his finances, estates issues, and final wishes in order. What remained, and what he sought my help to address, were unresolved family issues. He wanted to have peace in his family, or at least the opportunity for peace, as part of the legacy he left behind. As he said to me, "I came into the world well. I want to finish well." There is a process to finishing well—to being purposeful in how we design the closing chapters of our lives. This client came to me because he wanted to learn this process and to finish his life story with purpose and deliberateness.

■

There are so many decisions to be made around aging, illness, and end-of-life issues. We tend to put off those decisions until it's too late. We are so purposeful with how we plan for most of our lives. We study in school for careers that we want. We plan our families, our vacations, our homes, and our social lives. We cultivate friendships, relationships, and partnerships. Many people are so deliberate as to regularly develop five-year or even ten-year plans to guide them through the middle of their stories. But despite our endless planning, goal setting, and striving in the middle, we very often leave the last piece of our lives, the last chapter, undefined, leaving ourselves and our loved ones in a position to be reactive rather than proactive.

Here are some sobering realities for a country where (according to AARP statistics) ten thousand baby boomers reach retirement age every day. Statistics show that 90 percent of people say that talking about end-of-life care is important, but only 27 percent of people have actually had these conversations. Eighty-two percent of people say it's important to put their wishes in writing, but only 23 percent have actually done it. Eighty percent of people say that if seriously ill, they would want to talk to their doctor about end-of-life care, but only 7 percent of people say that they have had that discussion (AARP 2015).

These statistics were saddening to me but not surprising. Clearly, there is a need that these statistics highlight. I wrote this book to try to address that need and to help people who desperately want to have the important conversations around end of life do so. This book is meant to provide the tools, thought-provoking stories, and guiding questions for people to draft their life stories and finish well.

In addition, while there isn't a study to capture the percentage, I have sat with scores of people at the end of their lives, and in most cases that I have seen, people were dying with personal, financial, and relational issues that are unresolved. As a result, families were forced to make last-minute decisions without any knowledge of what the dying person wanted. Often, these decisions led to increased suffering for the patient and literally tore families apart. It has become clear that planning and having critical conversations ahead of time could have saved countless hours, regrets, challenges, and even dollars for these people and their families.

Perhaps even more importantly, people are ending their lives with experiences, life lessons, and stories unshared that will be lost to their families and generations to come because they ran out of time. This can be especially difficult if we do not plan ahead and share our stories with purpose every single moment because we never know the exact time and place when our final chapters will end. In general, we spend so much of our lives busy, preoccupied, and full of planning, but we don't plan or even realize how important it is to prepare for the last chapter of the stories of our lives. We don't even realize how helpful it can be and how much of a blessing it can be to ourselves and our families to take the time to capture our stories and prepare for the day of our passing. When we know how we want our stories we read, we choose more consciously who we want to be.

The purpose of this book is to help us choose our endings with as much care and purposefulness as we choose the rest of our lives so that we can finish well just as we have lived well. The first section of this book will outline the specific items needed to put legal affairs in order. I will provide information on beneficial legal documents for this chapter of life. I will help you organize necessary papers and information so that they are readily available for family and friends. This part of the book is the necessary, albeit unglamorous, work that is required to move forward with peace of mind.

The second section of this book will provide a format and suggestions for discussions and decisions around health care wishes and end-of-life decisions. I will help take the guesswork out of what you or a loved one *might* want regarding health care and end-of-life decisions so that wishes are clear and can be honored. I will discuss ways to have purposeful communication between loved ones regarding issues around health, aging, dignity, death, and dying. I will outline the questions that must be answered so that you can develop a success plan, not just a solutions plan.

The third part of this book strives to help facilitate conversations with loved ones. Whether there is a need to build bridges or heal old hurts, there are tools to create as positive an experience as possible with the people in your lives. This section will focus on relationships, or the list of characters in your life story who are most important to you.

The final section of the book provides a guide for leaving behind the items, stories, information, and wisdom that you would like to pass on to the next generation. You will reminisce, ponder, decide, and choose the stories and wisdom that you wish to live forever. Then you will write or record them in order to create your legacy.

■ ■ ■

There are so many things in this stage in life that are cause for celebration. I would like to provide a joyful opportunity to share those things—to connect more deeply with yourself and others. I would like for this book to help you write your own story—to be an opportunity to preserve for your friends and family your wishes, your memories, and your stories—so that you can gift to your children and loved ones a story that connects them to their past and to pass on the legacy that is your story.

And the people I write about throughout this book, what, ultimately, did these people teach me? They taught me that life is a book, and we write our own chapters in the book that is uniquely us and that ultimately the book closes with finality and gets put on a shelf with the bindings of those who have gone before us. Each chapter is beautiful and painful and unique and glorious because it is how we lived and who we are. In witnessing their endings, these people all taught me to live. They taught me that every moment matters. They taught me to be purposeful and intentional in how I write my own book. They taught me that I live forever in how my chapters impact others and in the way I choose to leave a mark on the world. At the same time, they taught me that I too will close my book someday. I really hope that someone sits beside me at that time with wonder at my story.

I hope that through this book I can share some of what I have learned and help you consider what the final chapters of your book will hold. I hope that you enjoy the process of sharing your past as well as determining your future. I hope that it provides opportunities to deepen the strong relationships that you have and heal the ones that might be tender. Mostly, I hope this book helps you accomplish whatever it is you need to put your heart and mind at rest, and that allows you to do the really meaningful stuff that really matters to you.

I believe that your life is your story and that you have the power to write it the way that you want. I believe our stories live on in everything we say and everything we do. I believe stories are immortal. I believe we should actively write our stories all the way to the end. Living fully and purposefully now keeps us from having regrets later. I write this guide so that we can live purposefully, fully, and without regret and finish well.

Chapter 1

Legal Considerations: Organization Matters

If Moses had gone to Harvard Law
School and spent three years working
on the Hill, he would have written
the Ten Commandments with three
exceptions and a saving clause.
—CHARLES MORGAN

I know. Talking about legal documents is boring and cumbersome. When people start talking legal documents, my eyes glaze over. No offense to lawyers (they're good people too), but the thought of visiting one to fill out the necessary forms ranks right up there with root canals and filing taxes. But the truth is, the alternative—not having the legal paperwork in order at the end of one's life—is much worse than going through the necessary steps. If you don't choose what you want done and who speaks for you when you are not able, then the courts will choose someone for you. In this case, you greatly reduce your chances of having your own personal wishes followed. If you don't have a Will, your estate will likely be tied up in court for a very long time. If you don't make decisions around your end-of-life care, then it is likely that the people making decisions for you will err on the side of life and the assumption that you might want everything done to try to save your life. In my career and personal life, I have seen much conflict around the guesswork about what a seriously ill person might want done for her when she can't speak for herself and what a deceased person might have wanted if he had left his wishes known, especially concerning funerals and passing on wealth and possessions.

My mother died this year. She did the best job she knew how to have legal documents in order. She had a Will and a handwritten note outlining her wishes. However, she was missing some important documents. Hers was not a large estate, and as a result of her minimal estate planning, her house and belongings were tied up in probate for six months. During this time, my siblings and I had to keep up the house and all the expenses, including maintenance, taxes, insurance, and utilities. We had to pay an attorney to move the process of selling her home and possessions through court. As I write this, it is January of the next year, and my siblings and I are finally just beginning to see the end of the process. This is only one example, albeit a benign one, of the consequences of not having one's legal paperwork in order at the end of life. What is passed down to others, meant to be a gift of generosity, can get wrapped up in confusion, hassle, and expense.

The best reason, however, for having your legal affairs in order is for your own protection and for the protection of your estate. For example, if you do not choose someone to take care of you and your affairs should you be unable to do so, a court could appoint someone to do that for you. If this happens, the court holds hearings and requires examinations. All parties hire lawyers, and the court makes an ultimate decision about who will be responsible for you. One attorney described this as "a lengthy, complex, ugly, adversarial process that few families can recover from."

Different states use different terms, but in many states, this decision-making position is referred to as guardianship or conservatorship. It is possible that the appointed guardian might even be a complete stranger. Yet, that guardian, conservator, or whatever title your state uses would make decisions for you and have control over your money, your home, and how your health care is handled. The court also determines the range of power granted to the guardian. In many cases, a guardian can make decisions on where you live, who you see, and your day to day activities. Conservators often take care of handling finances, paying bills, and managing property, including buying and selling real estate.

While many court-appointed guardians and conservators are doing wonderful work and are doing their best, journalist Ann Brenoff writes about how the court-appointed system fails repeatedly. According to Brenoff's reporting, there is nominal training, very little oversight or accountability, and great potential for abuse and fraud (Brenoff 2017). It is well worth you choosing your caregiver in advance of need.

Guardians are not the only potential source of abuse. The National Council on Aging reports that as many as five million elders are abused each year. Abuse includes physical abuse, neglect, emotional abuse, verbal abuse, sexual abuse, and financial abuse. Up to one in five older Americans has been financially exploited in the form of misusing or withholding an older adult's resources, and the annual loss to these victims is $2.6 billion to $36.5 billion. Sadly, most of the abuse is at the hands of family members (NCOA 2015). By every single recommendation, having secure legal documents and choosing your caregivers now are the best ways to decrease the potential for abuse and to avoid future legal problems.

Following is a list of necessary legal documents, what they are, why everyone needs them, and what can go wrong without them. Most people are familiar with the concept and understand the importance of a final will, but there are more documents that are helpful to ensure the outcome you want.

It is important to note that this chapter is not legal advice. For legal advice, please speak with an attorney, but hopefully, this information can give you an idea of where to start.

■■■ Documents

Will

The Will is a legal document that has two main purposes: to choose an executor and to describe your final wishes for how your estate should be distributed after you die. The executor is the person who is responsible for *executing* your wishes, or the person responsible for seeing that your wishes are carried out as stated in the Will. Without a Will, you die *intestate*. That sounds like a serious abdominal problem, but in reality, it is a serious problem for everything that you worked for and wish to pass on. It can also cause problems for your heirs and loved ones. In the event that you die intestate, your assets go into a lengthier probate, where your state's intestacy laws determine how to pay your debts and distribute your assets according to local survivorship laws. Your things do not get distributed by your choice or your heirs' choices but as the law describes. This is costly, incredibly time consuming, and a great source of conflict among families. If your ultimate desire is to have time and lawyers receive the bulk of your life's accumulations, then not having a Will is a great start.

With a Will, the probate court attempts to honor the instructions stated in the Will and resolve any challenges to those instructions. Your named executor is given power by the court to pay your debts and transfer your assets to your named beneficiaries. Small estates may be eligible for expedited procedures.

States vary in what is legally acceptable as a Will. While there are several online companies you might consider researching that will allow you to create a formal will, there is value in having an experienced estate-planning attorney advise you on your options and draft your state-specific document for you. Some states recognize handwritten wills, while others do not. It is important to check with an attorney to understand your state's requirements.

Do not forget to include intellectual property and social media accounts as assets in your Will.

Living Revocable Trust

The purpose of a living revocable trust is to retain control of your assets while you're alive and to appoint a trustee to transfer assets directly to your beneficiaries after you are deceased, allowing the bulk of your estate to avoid probate. The trustee will take care of your remaining financial obligations and see to it that your assets are disbursed as you wish them to be.

Without a living revocable trust, your entire estate goes through probate. This is what happened to my mother's estate. Without the trust, her house was in her name, and although the Will gave it to her three children, a probate proceeding was required so the court might appoint an executor with the authority to transfer estate assets. We hired a lawyer to petition the court and handle the probate proceedings for us. There was a mandatory waiting period for creditors and anyone else to make claims on the estate. Finally, after the legal process—a period of seven months—debts were paid, assets were distributed, and the court released her estate from probate.

When you create a trust, the trust owns your assets. After you die, the trust lives on and may continue to pay debts and transfer assets. A trust needs to be properly funded to work. You need to transfer ownership and title of all of your assets from your own name to the trust name. The need for a trust depends on what your financial goals are, the types of assets you have, and what state you live in. Again, you will need to discuss your assets and goals with an attorney. There are significant state-to-state differences in requirements for trusts.

Living Will

In many states, the living will has been replaced by advance directives (see the chapter on health care). The living will/ advance directive is designed to state your preferences for end-of-life medical treatment and your overall care and comfort in the case that you become incapacitated or terminally ill and are unable to make or communicate medical decisions yourself. When you cannot state your decision, your surrogate decision maker will make medical decisions on your behalf. Without your written guidance in an advance directive, your surrogate will base decisions on the care he or she believes you would wish to receive (called substituted judgment), or what he or she believes to be in your best interest. Courts and decision makers who don't know what you want will likely have little choice but to err on the side of life, doing everything possible to keep you alive.

Health Care Power of Attorney

A health care power of attorney names your surrogate decision maker, the person you trust with the final say about your medical care if you become incapacitated or seriously injured and cannot make or communicate your own medical decisions.

If you don't designate an agent under a health care power of attorney, many states default to laws that dictate who can make medical decisions on your behalf. Such statutes generally begin by designating next of kin, without any way of knowing whether that person is appropriate, and then work through a list of persons not as close, often ending with clergy or physicians. Other states may require appointment of a guardian or conservator of the person to make decisions for you. If conflicts arise among relatives, the battle over who gets to make decisions could go to court, and your conservator or guardian may be appointed by the court. That person could possibly even be a stranger.

Financial Power of Attorney

A financial power of attorney is much like a health care power of attorney but grants someone permission and authority to manage your finances. Your agent is to act financially only for your benefit and owes you a fiduciary duty; he or she does not own any of your assets. This authority can include handling your Social Security, insurance benefits, and salary; making payments; cashing checks; paying debts; managing investments; buying or selling real estate; and managing other financial interests. When creating the legal document, you may grant limited or expansive powers. Depending on your state and the language of the power of attorney, it may be effective immediately (although you would not give up any powers), begin only upon proof of your future incapacity, or end when you are incapacitated, or be effective for only a specified time period. An attorney can help you understand these options.

Without a financial power of attorney, no one can access your financial accounts or pay bills on your behalf. This could put you behind on meeting your financial obligations, possibly leading to increased debt. Without this, next of kin have no rights to access or manage your finances. If you fail to plan by executing a financial power of attorney, your family will likely need to go through a court process to have you declared incapacitated and to have a guardian or conservator of the estate appointed to handle your finances.

Supported Decision-Making

Supported decision-making is a legal document that is an alternative to guardianship if someone's physical or mental status is impaired. It is a way to support a person making his or her own decisions without removing that person's rights. While only a few states recognize supported decision-making, people with this document name someone to help them make the decisions *with* them rather than *for* them. You can use friends, family, and professionals to help you understand the situations and choices so that you can make your own decisions without the need for a guardian.

Retaining self-determination and decision-making results in increased independence, increased health, and increased ability to recognize and resist abuse. As the National Guardianship Association states in its Position Statement on Guardianship, "Alternatives to guardianship, including supported decision making, should always be identified and considered whenever possible prior to the commencement of guardianship proceedings." Supported decision-making recognizes that everyone has the right to make choices to the maximum of his or her ability, that people can get help exercising their rights to make choices without giving them up, and that there are many ways to get help making choices. Work with supporters to develop a plan identifying the areas where you might receive support, who will provide that support, and how it will be done. Supported decision-making recognizes, respects, and protects your right to make choices for as long as you are able. It can be added to your medical advance directive.

Supported decision-making is an excellent and respectful

tool when someone can participate in the decision-making process with assistance. If someone has a progressive illness where decisional capacity is anticipated to decrease over time and currently has the ability to knowingly execute legal documents, it would be prudent to also execute powers of attorney (health care and financial) as well as an advance directive in preparation for a possible time when the individual may no longer be able to make decisions, even with support. The supporters cannot act independently.

An example of this situation might be a person with dementia who, in the early stages of the disease, may function well when making decisions with caring support but who, in later stages of the disease, may need a surrogate to make all medical and financial decisions.

You can find tools for supported decision-making in the chapter "Additional Tools for Your Journey."

Designated Beneficiary Accounts

You will need legal advice in determining the need for designated beneficiary accounts. Designated beneficiary accounts give the people you name access to specified accounts at the time of your death. This is a way to keep assets out of probate. Having designated beneficiary accounts may help ensure your beneficiaries can easily file a claim and receive any benefits you've left in their names on bank accounts, life insurance policies, retirement funds, and annuity accounts. Some states even permit real estate deeds to designate beneficiaries. Assets for which you can designate beneficiaries pass outside your estate, so be sure you intend to leave that entire asset to the named beneficiary. He or she does not need to share.

Copy of Marriage Licenses, Divorce Decrees, Death Certificates, Military Paperwork, and Discharge Papers

Copies of all of these are important to transfer ownership of assets to a surviving spouse.

They are critical for establishing (or disproving) spousal benefits and entitlements.

Copy of Latest Federal Tax returns, Accountant Name, and Contact Information

This information will help your agent file your taxes if you become incapacitated or to file a final tax return after you die.

Without it, your taxes could be filed late, incurring penalties and liens.

Financial Accounts

Financial accounts help identify what banks and other financial institutions you do business with to pay bills or distribute assets.

Without this information clearly organized, bills may go unpaid and asset distributions could be delayed. Designating your bank accounts "transferable on death" to specific beneficiaries keeps them out of probate.

Life Insurance, Burial Insurance, Long-term Care Insurance, and Medical Insurance

Many insurance benefits go unclaimed because families, surrogates, and executors don't know the policies exist or can't find them. Make a list with policy name, policy number, issuing company, and company contact numbers. If possible, place copies of the policies or insurance certificates in your file.

Letter of Instruction/Intent

A letter of instruction gives your executor clear directions on how to manage/distribute your estate after your death.

Important items to include in a letter of intent include personal property assignments; pet care wishes; passwords and log-in information; where to find titles, deeds, and other paperwork, contact information and names of your lawyer, accountant, and other professionals; safe-deposit box and key location; Social Security number; birth certificates for you and minor children; and other key paperwork.

Your estate will be distributed according to the gifts designated in your will or trust. Your letter of instruction with its level of detail will be very helpful to your executor but be sure to also spell out your gifts in your estate plan documents. The Will and/or trust control distribution when there is a question about what goes to whom. Without a clear estate plan, your loved ones, even those with the best of intentions, will be in a free-for-all in an attempt to fulfill your final wishes.

Business Succession Plan

A business succession plan outlines what should happen to your business and who should be in control if you die or become incapacitated.

Without a succession plan, your business (and your employees) could suffer financially, and operations might be impacted. Ideally, your business should have its own living trust, separate from a personal trust, with a special trustee named to keep things running smoothly.

Documents to include in your business file include certificates of ownership, operating licenses, titles or deeds to real property, contracts, stocks/investments, articles of incorporation, bylaws, emergency plans, etc.

Funeral Plans

Funeral plans are necessary to make it clear what kind (if any) of memorial service you want and how you want your physical remains to be honored.

Though a funeral plan is not a legal document, it makes your loved ones' lives much easier if they know what your wishes are. You may want to prepay your funeral plan if possible. If you've pre-purchased a burial plot, cremation, or other services, you'll want to leave a copy of this information behind in a place where loved ones can easily find it. Some states have a special power of attorney, sometimes called an agent for the disposition of the remains. We will discuss funerals and end-of-life celebrations further in another chapter.

▪▪▪ Steps for Getting Your Affairs in Order

> I am my choices. I cannot not
> choose. If I do not choose,
> that is still a choice. If faced
> with inevitable circumstances,
> we still choose how we are
> in those circumstances.
> —JEAN PAUL SARTRE

In order to finish well, we need to prepare well. There are hoops that we have to jump through, as much as we don't want to, in order to get the results that we want.

The first thing you should do is put your important papers and copies of legal documents in one place. You can set up a computer file, put everything in a desk or dresser drawer, or list the information and location of papers in a notebook. If your papers are in a bank safe-deposit box, keep copies in a file at home. Check each year to see if there's anything new to add.

Next, make sure to tell a trusted family member or friend where you put all of your important papers. You don't need to tell this friend of family member about your personal affairs, but someone should know where you keep your papers in case of an emergency.

Below is a list of important personal and financial information to get in order.

Personal Records:

- ☐ full legal name

- ☐ Social Security number

- ☐ legal residence

- ☐ date and place of birth

- ☐ names, addresses, and phone numbers of spouse and children

- ☐ location of birth and death certificates and certificates of marriage, divorce, citizenship, and adoption

- ☐ driver's licenses

- ☐ employers and dates of employment

- ☐ education records

- ☐ military records, including discharge papers

- ☐ location of living will, health care proxies, Will, and other legal documents

- ☐ names, addresses, and telephone numbers of healthcare professionals

☐ hospital of choice, including address and phone number

☐ medications taken regularly, including dosages, name(s) of prescribing physician(s), and pharmacy phone number (be sure to update this regularly)

☐ names and phone numbers of religious contacts

☐ membership in groups and awards received

☐ names and phone numbers of close friends, relatives, doctors, lawyers, and financial advisors

☐ passwords for computer, phone, and accounts

☐ social media accounts and their passwords

☐ listings of intellectual properties

☐ funeral plans

Financial Records:

☐ sources of income and assets (including pension from your employer, IRAs, 401(k), interest, etc.)

☐ insurance information (life, health, long-term care, home, car) with policy numbers and agents' names and phone numbers (lots of life insurance goes unclaimed)

☐ names of your banks and account numbers (checking, savings, credit union)

☐ investment income (stocks, bonds, property) and stockbrokers' names and phone numbers

☐ copy of most recent income tax return

☐ location of most up-to-date Will with an original signature

☐ liabilities, including property tax (what is owed, to whom, and when payments are due)

☐ mortgages and debts (how and when they are paid)

☐ mineral and gas rights

☐ land leases

☐ cemetery deeds

☐ location of original deed of trust for home

☐ car title and registration

☐ credit and debit card names and numbers

☐ location of safe-deposit box and key (be sure to include the name on the account of the person or people who you want to access the box)

☐ other assets: location of titles, documents, ownership and current value of property, including automobiles, boats, inheritances, precious gems, collectibles, cemetery deeds, household items, hidden valuables, items in storage, and outstanding loans to family members and friends

☐ other liabilities: creditor institutions including their address and phone number, as well as approximate debt of mortgages, personal loans, credit cards, notes, IOUs, and other debts

While some of these records need to be physical, like a birth certificate, others, including contact information, a copy of your Will, and property information, can be digital. However, I recommend also having a hard copy of all of your lists and papers. Keep everything organized in a folder together and let at least one other significant, trusted person know where everything is located. Also, be sure to review your legal documents at regular intervals to see if there is a need for any changes or cancellations.

As researcher Brené Brown reminds us, "Clear is kind. Unclear is unkind" (Brown 2018). Being clear with our wishes is a kindness to ourselves and our loved ones who will carry out our wishes after we have passed. Careful planning now can help prevent unnecessary family conflict in the future by being clear about our wishes. In doing so, we will be setting ourselves and others up to succeed. Our wishes will be honored, and there is peace in that knowledge.

---■■■---

Chapter 2

Health Care Decisions: Your (Quality of) Life Depends on It

Our ultimate goal, after all, is not a good
death, but a good life to the very end.
—ATUL GAWANDE, *BEING MORTAL*

Just as there are important legal documents that you should get in order before end of life, it is important to consider and document health care decisions before you find yourself in a position where such decisions need to be made. Thinking deeply about your wishes surrounding health care and discussing these with your significant others, as well as formally writing them down, will help ensure that your needs are met and your desires are respected. This can help avoid a great deal of pain and confusion for you and your loved ones.

Here are several important documents that you should consider to legally document your end-of-life health care decisions. As with the previous chapter, it is important to note that this chapter is not legal advice but is information meant to give you an idea where to start.

■■■ Documents

Advance Directive

These days, when you go to the hospital or even to your doctor, one of the first questions you are asked is, "Do you have an advance directive?" An advance directive is a legal document that tells your doctor and family what kind of medical care you want if you can't tell them yourself. That is, if you have been seriously injured, are in the advanced stages of a disease, have severe dementia, are in a coma, or for any reason cannot speak for yourself, you have already made the hard decisions about what kind of care you want.

Your advance directive describes what kinds of treatments you do or do not want and what you want your care to look like. This can include whether you ever want to be put on a machine to breathe for you, if you want to be fed through a tube in your stomach if you are unable to eat, what kind of comfort measures you would like for pain control if you are dying, at what point you might not want to be transported to a hospital for more care, whether you might want to die at home, and whether you want to be an organ donor.

It is helpful to make these life decisions by writing a statement of your goals and values—who you are and what's important to you. You might also consider having a trial period of treatment before making a final decision on whether to reject a particular treatment. Remain flexible. Be willing to revisit all of your decisions as you walk through the process.

Supported Decision-Making

As discussed in detail in the previous chapter, in some states, supported decision-making may also be included in your advance directive. This articulates who you wish to help you make decisions regarding your health care, especially if you have a disability. An example of supported decision-making could look like this:

> My agent will work with me to make decisions and give me the support I need and want to make my own health care decisions. This means my agent will help me understand the situations I face and the decisions I have to make. Therefore, at times when my agent does not have full power to make health care decisions for me, my agent will provide support to make sure I am able to make health care decisions to the maximum of my ability, with me the final decision maker.

Durable Health Care Power of Attorney (DPA)

Durable power of attorney for health care is the document that names who will make decisions for you if you should become unable to make or communicate health care decisions yourself. It is critically important to have had conversations with this person (or people) to make clear what your wishes are regarding what you want your health care treatment to look like.

Physician Orders for Life-Sustaining Treatment (POLST)

Physician orders for life-sustaining treatment are a set of orders by your physician or an advanced practitioner that gives directions for your care if you should need emergency care. Often, POLST is done for people who are diagnosed with a terminal illness. It is filled out by your doctor after having a conversation with you about what kind of treatment you want if you become seriously ill. The doctor (or other advanced health care provider) writes physician orders, directing that your wishes be carried out when you are unable to speak for yourself. Its purpose is to provide medical orders to emergency personnel based on your current medical situation. This may include whether to start CPR (cardiopulmonary resuscitation) if you are found not breathing or without a pulse, whether you should go to the hospital for treatment, whether you should be put on a breathing machine, or whether you should be made as comfortable as possible where you are. It is important to note that this form must be signed by a physician or advanced practitioner in order to be carried out.

This term and the concept vary from state to state. Be sure to talk to your physician about this.

Do Not Resuscitate Order (DNR) and Allow Natural Death (AND)

A Do Not Resuscitate order (DNR) in some states is referred to as Allow Natural Death (AND) order. You may choose to state your preferences about cardiopulmonary resuscitation (CPR) in your advance directive. If you do not wish to have CPR done if your heart stops or you stop breathing, a doctor can write this order when you are hospitalized. You might also need a separate, out-of-the-hospital DNR order in case you are found not breathing and without a pulse at the place where you reside. Some people attach a copy to their refrigerators or place the order inside a container where it is readily found by medics. Most people say they do not want extraordinary measures in order to be kept alive if their hearts should stop beating or they stop breathing, yet without that order, medics are required to proceed with resuscitation measures.

Different states have different requirements, so check with your doctor and attorney.

■■■ Quality of Life: What Matters to You?

Now that you know some of the health care decisions you should be thinking about making before you are in a position to need them, we have to consider the hard question: How do you make these decisions? Though this decision-making process is deeply personal, here are some considerations to guide you.

First, you need to decide what is important to you while you are alive. What are the things you like to do? What gives quality and value to your life? In other words, what kind of quality of life is important to you? *Quality of life can be defined by being as healthy as you can and living as meaningfully as you can under your specific circumstances.* That meaning is defined by you.

An important thing to keep in mind is the "under the specific circumstances" part of the definition of quality of life. Of course, all of us would like to be perfectly healthy, able-bodied, and of sound mind, but that is not the point of thinking about what kind of quality of life you want. Instead, think about things that you absolutely cannot imagine life without, even in imperfect circumstances. Is being able to eat solid food important to you because food gives you joy? Will you be able to sacrifice other comforts as long as you can go outside on a sunny day because you can't imagine a life without nature? Or are you willing to endure any physical pain as long as you have your mental capacity and can recognize your loved ones? Where do you want to live? How much treatment, testing, blood work, or therapy are you willing to undergo? In other words, think about what makes life worth living to you; what is most important to you; and what makes life fulfilling, satisfying, and joyful in order to get to the heart of the quality of life you need.

Of course, making these decisions is extremely difficult and makes many people uncomfortable. We don't like to think about ourselves in a weakened, vulnerable state. Ultimately, in making these decisions, we must come to understanding and conversation around our own mortality. We must be willing to have honest, open conversations with our loved ones about what is important to us, what our fears are, and *especially* what realistic expectations are given our prognosis. You see, here is the reality: We are all dying. We are all dying! (Go ahead, try saying it.) When we are aware of this fact of life, when we accept it, we can plan for that death so that we may put the fears around death behind us and live our lives fully.

In so many situations, and especially at the end of life, denial is the biggest enemy. Time and time and time again, I have seen people faced with a serious diagnosis, accident, or injury to themselves or a loved one, and they spend so much time stuck in a place of fear and disbelief. When this happens, decisions are made out of a place of weakness, panic, and fear. Families are torn and agonize over making decisions that they have not been prepared to make, and in their ambivalence and unknowing, they often choose treatments that result in painful procedures that have very little chance of results that improve a patient's life.

In order to make decisions from a sound, authentic place with clarity and knowledge, we need to have these conversations ahead of time. We need to be willing to be realistic in our expectations. We are going to die. We cannot stop that from happening. Understanding that aging and death are inevitable helps us live as fully as possible, up to our last moment, rather than spend our precious time and energy fighting the inevitable. We need to make peace with death in order to live fully and without regret.

As great reading on this subject, I recommend that *everyone* read *Being Mortal* by Atul Gawande. In this brilliant book, Gawande describes the medical system, the long-term care system, the process of aging, and the breakdown that our bodies go through as we age (Gawande 2014).

A long career in health care gave me witness to countless experiences of families struggling to make life-and-death decisions when family members were at the terminal stages of illness or injury. I don't think I can find the words to describe the agony that loved ones go through, walking the line between trying to decide what their beloved may want in any situation and willingness to let go. Most of us have probably been in this situation and have been a part of making those difficult decisions when we have a loved one who is dying. This process is never easy. We know that it is excruciating. On the other hand, I have seen families and friends who are confident and at peace during the same painful scenarios. This happens when they know, with relative certainty, that no matter what the decisions are that they need to voice, they are honoring the decisions of the individuals who are no longer able to speak for themselves. It is gratifying and rewarding to know that you are helping someone finish out his or her story the way that person has chosen.

I am sometimes haunted by memories of the struggles I have seen patients and families go through. Many of those people changed my life and shaped my worldview, though they will never know. I would like to share the story of one of those patients with you now to elucidate what I am describing.

I was working in a trauma intensive care unit (ICU) at a large teaching hospital. Our unit also took care of surgical intensive care patients, and I tended to care for the same patients each time I worked. I liked the continuity of care that I could give them, and I liked forming a deep relationship with the patients and their families. At the time of this story, I had been working in the ICU for several years, so I saw a lot of people with end-stage illnesses and terminal medical problems with no chance of returning to anywhere near their former functioning and many with very little chance of survival.

Despite the odds being stacked against them, many families and patients I met wanted everything to be done. For me, hearing this directive was sometimes heart-wrenching. In the medical system, I saw how we put people through so much pain and suffering just to keep them alive. Indeed, it is what patients and families often expect and demand—that no matter what, the health care system should keep people alive and ultimately should be able to cure anything.

This particular patient who comes to mind was a middle-aged man with a condition known as necrotizing pancreatitis. In a healthy person, the pancreas secretes enzymes for digestion. With this disease, the enzymes are released into the abdomen, and the body is literally digesting itself. In an effort to treat his disease, the man had surgery to open his abdomen. He was kept deeply medicated to control pain and was on a ventilator to breath for him. We did dressing changes to his abdomen a couple times a day to try to allow him to heal from the inside.

Despite our best efforts, every day this man became sicker and sicker. Infection set in, so we tried to treat the infection with antibiotics. His system went into shock. We had him on medication to increase his blood pressure and control his heart rate gave him blood transfusions. And still, every day he continued to get worse. His family came in regularly to receive updates on his condition, and they asked for everything to be done. So, at the family's request, we continued care—open abdomen, dressing changes, ventilator, medications, IV feeding, etc.

As the man continued toward dying, I asked myself, "Why are we doing this to you?" Even then, I knew the answer was simple. The family wanted to know that everything possible had been done to try to save their loved one. And so, the days went on with the man's condition only worsening. One day, the family came to see this man, and I will never, ever forget this moment. Upon seeing her father, the patient's daughter began to sob. She threw herself over her father's distended abdomen and cried, "Oh, Daddy! Why are we doing this to you?"

In this moment, I became overwhelmed by emotion. This man's daughter had asked the question I had asked so many times. "Why are we doing this to you?" I turned away and began to sob silently. My best friend at the time and fellow nurse saw my shoulders shaking. She led me away from the unit. I've never had a feeling like that in my life—not before and not since. I felt that I was sitting outside of myself and watching myself cry. I felt like the tears would never stop. I was crying for all the people who suffered through so much because their loved ones, truly doing what they thought was best for their family member, were afraid to let them go. I still tear up when I remember this story. My heart breaks for the families forced into these decisions and for the patients who suffer because of them.

Next, contrast this story with the recent death of Pam, a lab manager in a cancer research lab at a major university. Pam's personal story with cancer began twenty-seven years ago. She was diagnosed with a small tumor in her breast at the age of thirty-three and underwent a lumpectomy and radiation as well as chemotherapy. After this initial treatment, Pam thought she was cancer free, but two years later, her cancer returned, and she learned that this time the cancer had metastasized. Pam now had cancer in her chest wall and on the outside of her lung. She was thirty-five years old with two young children at home.

Armed with this information, Pam made the decision with her family and her husband, David, that she would pursue treatment. Pam had known other people who had tried to overcome cancer and had what she called "terrible deaths." Pam knew that, no matter what, she didn't want to "die a bad death" from the treatments. With this understanding of what kind of quality of life Pam could and could not accept, she chose to undergo a difficult treatment of a peripheral stem cell bone marrow transplant and high levels of chemotherapy.

For the next eleven years, Pam was cancer free, but Pam's cancer eventually returned. This time, she underwent different drug regimens and ultimately tried a risky clinical trial drug. Pam almost died from the medication, and she stopped the medication before the whole series was completed. Again, weighing her options and potential quality of life, Pam decided that this time she would not take any more medicine that would make her terribly sick, and she did not want to take a medication that had a less than 50 percent chance of killing her cancer cells. Again, armed with a clear decision about the quality of life she needed, Pam spent the next eight years in various cancer treatments, and she was well enough to work in the job she loved during most of this time.

Three years before Pam died, a friend of hers had died suddenly. The friend had not set her death up, and the bereaved husband was devastated. Seeing her friend and her friend's husband go through this terrible ordeal, Pam decided to face her death and take charge of what her death would look like. Again, she was committed to dying a good death, and she realized this meant planning ahead.

So, Pam and David went funeral shopping. They went to three different funeral homes and discussed, in detail, what Pam wanted. Having thought about her final wishes, Pam asked the funeral home they selected to place her ashes into thirty-one bags after her death. After a difficult but productive day, Pam and David celebrated with margaritas, and Pam made a list of thirty-one places she wanted her ashes to be placed. She designed a route for David to take his motorcycle across the country, delivering her ashes to the places she named. In addition, Pam knew she wanted to die at home, and she knew she didn't want to die in her own bed, so Pam and David fixed up another room at their house for when the time came when Pam was dying. David put bird feeders outside of the window.

In the meantime, Pam took up playing the ukulele. Every morning for the next three years, Pam and David went into this room, and Pam played the ukulele. They read the Bible together and meditated. Seven months before Pam died, she made a circle chart of the visitors she wanted to see. As her disease progressed and her condition deteriorated, only the people in the most inner circle would be allowed to visit her. Eight days before Pam died, friends in her inner circle came to visit. Pam was still active and cheerful. She assured her friends that she had done everything on her bucket list, but she said there was only one thing left that she'd always wanted to kind of do. She'd never rolled (toilet-papered) a yard! Her friends looked at her, surprised. No one in the group had rolled a house either, so the group decided to go and toilet-paper a nearby neighbor's yard. They had a blast. Six days before she died, Pam sat at the dining room table, played the ukulele, and sang "Happy Birthday" to her sister.

The day of Pam's death, her family was gathered around her and shared their favorite stories about her. Her clergywoman prayed for Pam and reassured her that the family was ready to let her go and that she could go in peace. Pam died forty-five minutes later, surrounded by the people she loved most. David says that, in the end, there was great peace in honoring what Pam wanted, for him, for Pam, and for all who cared about her. Pam had planned her funeral and planned a party at Gilda's club for after her death. She chose the music. She told everyone, "I'm going to be okay, and you're going to be okay." Together, Pam and David helped ensure that Pam would have her good death.

I love the concept of dying a good death, which Pam modeled for all of us so beautifully. It means that you get to choose how fully you are going to live while you are alive, even if you are dying. It also allows you to be purposeful at the end of your story, and in the end, there's great peace in that.

▪▪▪ A Note on Hospice Care

When most of us hear of someone moving into hospice care, we tend to think they are days or moments away from death. While that may be the case, the chronically ill or terminally ill person and family may choose hospice for care even if the death is estimated to be within six months. Contrary to popular belief, hospice care is not the same as giving up on a person. Simply, hospice care is defined as providing palliative care (focused on comfort and relief of symptoms) instead of curative care. The purpose of hospice is to provide emotional and spiritual support for the client and family as well as palliative and physical support to the client. Hospice care includes a team of people, nurses, social workers, clergy, and aides to help the transition from life to death be as peaceful and as personal as possible. I've heard so many stories from families who were surprised by how sacred and beautiful their experience was working with hospice and being present when their loved one died.

There is a difference in treatments between hospice care and palliative care choices. The terminology is different for billing and insurance purposes as well. While hospice foregoes all aggressive treatment, palliative care does not forego ongoing aggressive care.

I went to high school in a tiny little once-upon-a-town in Indiana. Forty years after graduation, I learned that my high school Spanish teacher was now living in Tennessee, not far from me, and that he was battling brain cancer. I went to visit him in the rehabilitation center after his craniotomy.

I walked in the hospital room and said, "Mr. D, I am Kim. You were my Spanish teacher in high school." He looked at me and said, "I know who you are."

I was stunned. Forty years and a brain tumor removed. Could he really know? I told him a story then. I told him that I had never thanked him for a time in high school when he had stepped up and fought for me to be part of a project that I badly wanted to be on. I thanked him for bringing his guitar to school and teaching us silly little songs about cockroaches and such during Spanish class. I thanked him for being patient and steadfast. He wept. So did I.

Shortly after that, Mr. D was placed in hospice care. I went to visit him every week. During these visits, I'd ask him about his life, and he would answer and cry. We talked about death and his fears. I had the sense that these conversations were freeing for him, putting into words the things he carried in his heart. He said to me once, "You know, Kim, these aren't all sad tears." I knew. They were love tears and gratitude tears and reflection tears and letting-go-of-fear tears. They were cathartic.

During one of my visits, I told him about this book I was writing. For our next visit, I told him I would bring a journal and interview him and then write his story for him so that he could gift it to his children and his grandchildren. He seemed to like this idea, and I was excited about putting this work into action. Here was something I could help him create, even while his health slowly faded. However, when I came back the next week, my teacher was in a coma. He died peacefully a week later.

I was grateful for the time I was able to spend with my dear teacher, and I was especially grateful that hospice offered him peace and dignity before his death.

In addition to thinking deeply about what meaning you need in your life and what quality of life is necessary for you, there are other considerations to think through and discuss in designing your story around health care choices.

If you have an underlying illness, understand your health condition as much as possible. To understand your health condition, you might:

☐ research the illness and treatment as well as the disease progression and the likely prognosis;

☐ bring a family member or loved one with you for doctor visits;

☐ make a list of questions;

☐ take notes;

☐ get a second opinion and more if needed; or

☐ find out the statistics behind the efficacy of your treatments.

While it is important to trust your health care providers, even more so, trust yourself with your decisions; remember that it is *your* life. Have this discussion about how the end of your life will look with the people who matter to you and decide how to come into a place of acceptance. As part of this movement toward acceptance, you might think about *who* you want to be moving forward, even as your illness progresses. This helps remind you that you are not your illness but so much more. You are still writing your story.

After your research, please remember that every one of us is different. Your journey may be unique from the research. How you respond to treatment will be different than how others respond because *you* are different. This is another time when it is helpful to remain flexible.

Below are some questions that you might ask yourself to guide you through this process of deciding what your final chapter will look like. After reflecting on what dying a good death means for you, write down your plan so that you, too, might have no regrets.

▨■▨ Thinking through Your End-of-Life Wishes

1. Regarding end-of-life treatments, what are your end-of-life goals?

2. Keeping in mind that your life is your story and, "You may not control life's circumstances, but getting to be the author of your life means getting to control what you do with them," (Atul Gawande), what do you want your death to look like?

3. If your heart stops, do you want CPR (cardiopulmonary resuscitation)? This includes chest compression, electric heart defibrillation (shocking), and mechanical ventilation.

4. Do you want to have a tube to help you breathe if your breathing becomes impaired (intubation)?

5. Do you want to be placed on a ventilator (breathing machine)?

6. If you are unable to eat due to mechanical problems or weakness, do you want a feeding tube placed?

7. Do you want IV fluids?

8. Do you want antibiotics if you develop an infection?

9. Is there a point when you do not want to be transported to a hospital to be evaluated and treated and would rather stay at your home, even if this means that you could get sicker and even die?

10. How much sedation / pain management do you want?

11. Who do you want present when you are dying?

12. What do you want your environment/surroundings to be like?

13. Who will make decisions for you when you no longer can?

14. What matters the most to you as you near the end of your life? How do you want to spend your last days?

15. Do you wish to be an organ donor? Which organs would you like to donate?

16. What picture comes to mind for you with the term "death with dignity"?

Once you have worked through these questions, it may be useful to think through the questions again under different scenarios: What if you had dementia? What if you were living in a nursing home? Would your answers be age-related? The goal of these questions is to decide what is or is not acceptable to you. If you are struggling, consider having these conversations with your family, trusted friends, and health care providers. In addition, mediators, counselors, conflict managers, communication coaches, and clergy can all help have these conversations.

You may need to revisit the questions above periodically as your situation changes or as you gain new information. You should be flexible and be willing to reexamine all of your decisions. Recheck them for *your* truth. Adjust your wishes, your yeses, and your noes accordingly.

These questions are hard and somewhat unpleasant to think about, yet addressing them as honestly and thoroughly as possible now will save you and your loved ones much unnecessary stress and pain when the time comes. Health care providers can also help with these conversations.

Chapter 3

It's My Party: Planning Your Celebration of Life

There'll be two dates on your tombstone
and all your friends will read them.
But all that is going to matter is
the little dash between them.
—KEVIN WELCH

I just returned from the funeral of an eighty-five-year-old woman. The funeral home was packed to standing room only with people of all ages. I looked at the program, which had two dates. The first, the date of her birth, was August 1933. The second date, September 30, 2018, was the date of her death. Between the dates was a dash. That dash, just a small horizontal line on a page, represented her whole life, her whole story. That dash was why friends and family were there to celebrate her.

Luckily for her family, this octogenarian spelled out her wishes for her funeral in detail well before her death. Her daughter told me that talking about her mother's funeral so far in advance was a little sad and a little odd, but in the end, it made everything so much easier. The daughter was able to bury her mother with no regrets or second-guessing, knowing that the ceremony was exactly as her mother had wanted. Her mother had chosen her casket, her favorite verse, her preacher, and all of her speakers. She wanted the family to set up a table of pictures of the family members who had gone to heaven before her. She wanted a video shown of her with her friends. She articulated how she wanted her funeral to be happy. She wanted no tears shed. As she was aging, this woman's family used to ask her if she needed anything. She always replied, "A million dollars." Her final funeral service request was for all who were present to dance to "I Want to Be a Millionaire." And we did dance. As her casket was wheeled out of the funeral parlor, we danced with joy and smiles and, yes, even amid tears.

I share this story with you to demonstrate that your funeral is your last opportunity to give a meaningful experience to your loved ones. By designing your funeral with care and thoughtfulness, you can guarantee that your wishes will be met and that your loved ones will celebrate you in the way you've always imagined. I sometimes hear people say, "I wonder what my funeral will be like." But by planning ahead, you don't have to wonder. You can design the experience that you want. If that includes dancing to pop tunes, sharing goofy photos, or inviting everyone in your life to travel to your favorite place in the world, then that's exactly how things should be.

▨■▨ Planning Your Party

So, why do funerals even matter? What function do they serve, and why have we, as humans, participated in funeral service for thousands of years? Dr. Alan Wolfelt writes, "Like all rituals, the funeral ritual, is a public, traditional and symbolic means of expressing our beliefs, thoughts and feelings about the death of someone loved" (Wolfelt 2016). I believe that funerals have been with us throughout history because they help us navigate the chasm between life and death in several key ways. First, funerals help us to say goodbye to those we love. With funerals, we take time to recognize the life, the presence, the significance, and the purpose of the person who died. Funerals also provide us an opportunity to sort through the myriad of emotions and thoughts we may have around this life we shared with the deceased. At funerals, we can express our gratitude, our joy, our pain, and the full complexity of our relationship with that person. We can, in a way, speak to them one last time.

Second, we are in communion with others sharing the same loss when we attend a funeral. We are present to support and be supported during a time of loss. We share stories, hopes, and grief. This communion is incredibly intimate and helps those involved know that they are not alone. Brené Brown writes that in her research on trust, showing up for funerals was one of the highest gifts of connection and trust building that a person could offer (Brown 2017). In other words, by showing up, we show that we care. We are there when it is difficult. This is a great act of respect and love.

All of this helps us to begin the healing process of finding a life without that person and finding a new normal of who we are now that this person is no longer present in body in our lives. Perhaps the greatest gift about a funeral, the thing that most amazes me, is that someone else dying helps us intensely and acutely appreciate our own lives. I have never left a funeral where I and others were not forced to consider our own mortality. Often, when confronted with this truth that we may usually avoid, we find ourselves immensely grateful. We vow, at least for a while, to hold our relationships dearer, to stop and smell the flowers, to appreciate the things that matter, and to live more fully. We recognize that our individual story will have an ending, and we become purposeful, at least for a moment, in writing who we will be in that story.

When I think back on events in my life, I find that I can recall so many details of the funerals I have been to, both as a child and as an adult. Indeed, the experience of funerals is so profound that we often remember the details of funerals more than many other events. Funerals are powerful social functions that bring people together, connecting them over a mutual loss. More and more over time, I have seen funerals move from somber, black-clothed, heavy events to family gatherings that, though incredibly sad at the loss of a loved one, are also celebrating the life and the memories of that individual.

In my own family, memories of funerals include tremendous grief and loss, followed by the family gathering for a meal with lots of talking, laughter, and memories. I'm a bit incredulous that some of our best family photos take place before or after funerals, but this is the case. As my own experience has taught me, funerals are more than mourning loss and celebrating life.

They are also one of the biggest gathering moments, bringing together entire families, friends, communities, and the many who have walked with us during different chapters of our lives.

While it might seem difficult to plan what you want your funeral to look like, it may be easier to think of it as planning your party. This is the celebration of your life! This is the final memory and gift that you will leave behind. In the book *Good Mourning*, Elizabeth Meyer and Caitlin Moscatello write, "Most people do not plan. What's changing is more people are talking about it, and the openness of the conversation. Our world will be a better place when people let their wishes be known" (Meyer and Moscatello 2015).

There are many benefits to planning your own celebration. Besides being the architect of your own ending, you are truly blessing those who are left behind. Sixth-generation funeral director Caleb Wilde discusses the things we should know that will help us see the importance of planning our celebrations. First, he writes, when friends and family are grieving, it is so difficult to make these kinds of decisions and all too easy to make bad financial decisions. When we plan ahead, we can determine exactly what we are willing to pay for. As an example, Wilde writes that between $800 and $1,200 is often spent on embalming, and embalming is not necessary for 70 to 80 percent of bodies that are embalmed.

Besides expense, it is impossible to assume what kind of service someone might have wanted. Unknowing can result in families fighting over their differences of opinion. Each person may think that he or she knows what the deceased person wanted, and each person will almost certainly have a different opinion. Unfortunately, I know of families who still carry guilt and worry over whether the service they planned for their loved one was done the *right* way. They carry this their whole lives.

In contrast to this, I have talked to people, like my story at the beginning of this chapter, who are so grateful that they did not have to make these difficult decisions about how to honor their loved ones. They could rest in knowing the service was exactly what the person wanted. They could spend their time saying goodbye and beginning the grief cycle without the extra worry and guilt. As one man told me with a laugh, "My mom laminated her funeral plans. Who does that? She did not want anyone to change her plans, and having those plans, really made the funeral so easy."

When planning your celebration, don't worry too much about tradition if that's not important to you, and instead, focus on what would align with your values and how you want your story to end. Funerals and their services are changing. Traditional services with embalming and caskets cost, on average, $9,000. However, more and more people are choosing other options. Funeral services with a body present are being replaced with celebrations of life where the body is not present. These services are livelier, life-centered, and focused around who the individual was and how he or she lived. They are quite different from the quiet, somber events that were traditional funerals and that we have likely all attended. At a celebration of life, stories are shared, favorite music is played, and pictures are displayed and passed around. They can take place anywhere—parks, ball fields, beaches, wherever best represents the deceased. I know a friend whose brother planned an all-day picnic for his funeral, followed by a big bonfire where he requested his ashes to be shot out of a cannon. Decades later, this man is immortalized as his brother continues to tell the story of that day to the amusement and amazement of his audience. Some people even celebrate living funerals. A living funeral has all of the components of a regular funeral, only the celebrated person gets to actively say goodbye as well as hear and share in his or her ending.

Though it may be less pleasant to think about, another important choice in your planning will be how you want your body to be handled. Rather than being squeamish, though, I recommend that you consider this decision another opportunity to align your final wishes with your values. Again, there is not just one *right* option, so to speak, and trends are shifting. Due to cost and concern for the environment, cremation is rapidly becoming a more popular alternative to traditional burial. Now, nearly half of American deaths lead to cremations, where that number was only around 28 percent in 2002. There are projections that cremation rates may rise to 80 percent by 2035, allowing people to hold a memorial whenever and wherever they choose and to keep or scatter the ashes as wished (NFDA 2018).

Green funerals are also becoming more popular. Rather than being embalmed and buried in caskets, some people are opting for burial in a biodegradable coffin or even a shroud. Another newer option is to be buried in a burial pod that will then provide nutrients to a tree growing above. This way, people become part of the natural system—literally ashes to ashes and dust to dust, becoming in their death part of the earth and giving new life. I think of my father, an outdoorsman and naturalist at heart, in his metal coffin and wonder if he would have embraced the opportunity for renewal and revitalization that the green funeral offers. There are many green funeral options, as the concept has gained popularity.

Be sure to select a funeral home or crematorium ahead of time. You will often be able to lock into selections for caskets, urns, and services, as well as prices ahead of time. Consider the options that feel right to you and bring you the most peace.

Another step that you may want to take in writing your ending is to literally write your ending—your obituary and/or your eulogy. This may be a thoughtful exercise in describing who you were, how you lived, and what was important to you. This is the perfect opportunity to articulate your legacy that you want to leave behind and to tell your story to those who will survive you. It is an ideal chance to reflect on your own journey through life and to leave your messages and wisdom for your loved ones. I like the idea of something in my own words being read to the people who gather to say goodbye to me. I like the idea of having my goodbye to offer them. There are many tips and formats online for writing obituaries and eulogies. These include help with deciding your style and theme. There are examples to help you get started. There is no wrong way to do this. It is your personalized message. One of my clients asked for help in writing his. I noted the important points that he wanted to say, chose the style (he wanted more lighthearted and humorous to reflect his personality), and then we crafted the message together.

Emily Phillips was a retired teacher in Florida who wrote her own obituary shortly before she died of pancreatic cancer on March 25, 2015 (Phillips 2015). In her words, as a touching tribute to her life:

It pains me to admit it, but apparently, I have passed away. Everyone told me it would happen one day but that's simply not something I wanted to hear, much less experience. Once again, I didn't get things my way! That's been the story of my life all my life. And while on that subject (the story of my life) ... on February 9, 1946 my parents and older sister celebrated my birth and I was introduced to all as Emily DeBrayda Fisher from Hazelwood. I can't believe that happened in the first half of the last century but there are records of file in the Court House which can corroborate this claim. Just two years later when another baby girl was born, I became known as the middle sister of the infamous three Fisher Girls, and the world was changed forever. As a child I walked to the old Hazelwood Elementary School where teachers like Mrs. McCracken, Mrs. Davis and Mrs. Moody planted the seed that eventually led me to becoming a teacher. I proudly started my teaching career at that same elementary school in January 1968, and from there I went on to teach young children in the neighboring states of Virginia, Georgia, as well as Florida where I retired after 25 years. So many things in my life seemed of little significance at the time they happened but then took on a greater importance as I got older. The memories I'm taking with me now are so precious and have more value than all the gold and silver in my jewelry box. Memories … where do I begin? Well, I remember Mother wearing an apron; I remember Daddy calling Square Dances; I remember my older sister pushing me off my tricycle (on the cinder driveway); I remember my younger sister sleep walking out of the house; I remember grandmother Nonnie who sewed exquisite dresses for me when I was little; I remember grandmother Mamateate wring a chicken's neck so we could have Sunday dinner. I remember being the bride in our Tom Thumb Wedding in first grade and performing skits for the 4-H Club later in grade five. I remember cutting small rosebuds still wet with dew to wear to school on spring mornings, and I remember the smell of newly mowed grass. I remember the thrill of leading our high school band down King Street in New Orleans for Mardi Gras (I was head majorette). I remember representing Waynesville in the Miss North Carolina Pageant, and yes, I twirled my baton to the tune of "Dixie." It could have been no other way. I married the man of my dreams (tall, dark, and handsome) on December 16, 1967 and from that day on I was proud to be Mrs. Charlie Phillips, Grand Diva Of All Things Domestic. Our plan was to have two children, a girl and a boy. Inexplicably we were successful in doing exactly that when we were blessed with our daughter Bonnie and then later our son Scott. Seeing these two grow into who they were supposed to be brought a wonderful sense of meaning to our lives. This might be a good time to mend fences. I apologize for making sweet Bonnie wear No Frills jeans when she was little and for "red-shirting" Scott in kindergarten. Apparently, each of these things was humiliating to them but both were able to rise above their shame and become very successful adults. I'd also like to apologize to Mary Ann for tearing up her paper dolls and to Betsy for dating a guy she had a crush on. Just when I thought I was too old to fall in love again, I became a grandmother, and my five grand-angels stole not only my heart, but also spent most of my money. Sydney Elizabeth, Jacob McKay, and Emma Grace (all Uprights) have enriched my life more than words can say. Sydney's "one more, no more" when she asked for a cookie: Jake saying he was "sick as a cat" when I'd said that someone was sick as a dog; and Emma cutting her beautiful long hair and then proceeding to shave off one of her eyebrows ... Yes, these are a few of my favorite things. They're treasures that are irreplaceable and will go with me wherever my journey takes me. I've always maintained that my greatest treasures call me Nana. That's not exactly true. You see, the youngest of my grand-angels, William Fisher

Phillips and Charlie Jackson Phillips call me "Nana Banana." (Thank you Chris and Scott for having such spunky children.) These two are also apt to insist that I "get their hiney" whenever I visit, and since I'm quite skilled in that area, I've always been able to oblige. (I actually hold the World's Record for "Hiney Getting," a title that I wear with pride.) Speaking of titles ... I've held a few in my day. I've been a devoted daughter, an energetic teenager, a WCU graduated (summa cum laude), a loving wife, a comforting mother, a dedicated teacher, a true and loyal friend, and a spoiling grandmother. And if you don't believe it, just ask me. Oh wait, I'm afraid it's too late for questions. Sorry.

So ... I was born: I blinked: and it was over.

No buildings named after me; no monuments erected in my honor. But I DID have the chance to know and love each and every friend as well as all my family members. How much more blessed can a person be? So, in the end, remember ... do your best, follow your arrow, and make something amazing out of your life. Oh, and never stop smiling.

If you want to, you can look for me in the evening sunset or with the earliest spring daffodils or amongst the flitting and fluttering butterflies. You know I'll be there in one form or another. Of course, that will probably comfort some while antagonizing others, but you know me ... it's what I do. I'll leave you with this ... please don't cry because I'm gone; instead be happy that I was here. (Or maybe you can cry a little bit. After all, I have passed away). Today I am happy and I am dancing. Probably naked.

Love you forever.

As I have emphasized again and again throughout this book, death is a given. While we cannot control, in most cases, how or when we die, we can control how we want to be remembered. Plan your celebration and have these conversations with your family and friends early. As you do, be creative, have fun, and be true to what feels right to you. Make your wishes as clear and precise as possible. It will bring you and your loved ones peace and will allow the memory of you to live through to the very end.

Things to Consider When Planning Your End-of-Life Ceremony

☐ Who will be in charge of executing your wishes?

☐ What, if any, type of religious preference do you have for the ceremony? Answering this question alone is most helpful, as not knowing this is one of the top sources of family conflict.

☐ Which particular funeral home or crematorium would you like to use?

☐ How do you want your body to be prepared?

☐ What do you want to wear or have with you to go to your final resting place?

☐ What type of funeral service/end-of-life celebration do you want?

☐ Where do you want your celebration to take place?

☐ Will there be a viewing?

☐ How long would you like the event to last?

☐ Who do you want to be present?

☐ What would you like read, said, or sung, and who should perform these acts?

☐ Who will write your obituary? What do you want to be sure it includes?

☐ Do you want any additional activities or gatherings after the funeral?

☐ Do you want to donate any or all of your remains for scientific use? If you would choose to donate your body to science, this decision must be made ahead of time and must be set up by you in advance of your death. It is not something that your family can do for you later.

Chapter 4

Telling Your Story

Owning our story and loving
ourselves through that process is the
bravest thing that we'll ever do.
— BRENÉ BROWN

In every moment, our actions and how we interact with those around us create an energy that passes through person to person in an endless ripple effect of impact and influence. These actions, how we choose to live in any given moment, and who we are, are the key components that make up the heart of the stories of our lives.

Why is it useful to think about our lives as stories? Simply because there is immense power in stories. Stories live forever, so stories make us immortal. Stories give sense, purpose, and narrative to our lives. At the same time, if our readers are open to the lessons that our pasts hold, stories allow others to learn, grow, and be changed by our experiences. As a friend of mine recently wrote, "Stories vanquish mortality. Every individual has a *story*; that rabbit trail-roller coaster adventure which has led each of us to where we are, and who we have become. Yet the lessons of that journey will pass with you, unless you pass it on." In order for the lessons of our lives to have meaning beyond ourselves, we *must* tell our stories.

Our stories are our legacies—the greatest gift that we can give to our loved ones. Think about someone you may have lost recently: a parent, a sibling, a friend. Were there things that you wish you knew about that person? A man I know attended the funeral of a lifelong friend. He penned these words afterward: "Don't you wish that when people pass on that their story will be heralded? So many stories never told. So many great things never learned. I know we have obituaries, but you cannot express a life in an obituary. I need to think about this. It troubles me" (Rene Verstraete).

I doubt that anyone has ever regretted having too rich a picture of someone who has passed away, too many stories, or too many memories. Sharing your story fully will give your loved ones a permanent part of you to hold onto.

To illustrate how stories can be a gift to others, I would like to share a story from a friend of mine who lost her father at a young age. My friend wrote:

> It is weird as an adult and parent how you realize you knew very little about your own parents while growing up; their marital problems, their friend issues, their worries about bill and their struggles, their ups and downs … While I know no human is without fault and cannot be perfect, I have nothing but the best memories

of my dad and how much he loved us. In my eyes and memories, he was the perfect Dad. I remember so much and so little at the same time, of my dad being sick and even this very day, December 19th, of when he passed from a battle with brain cancer. While he was so different, his love was the same. While his daily routine (and my mom's) drastically changed in a blink, they strived to protect our hearts and the things we could remember. To carry the things that came along with brain cancer would have been too much for a 10- and a 12-year-old.

Today marks 25 years since my dad passed away and there isn't a day I don't think about him. I remember leaving the hospital, sitting on my bed with my aunt, hearing a phone call, sitting at a funeral, and people at my house with food. But bigger and more important than that, I remember the tickle monster, I remember riding the lawn mower with him, I remember the tee ball team that he coached. I remember him coming home for lunch and watching All My Children. I remember the cigars outside. I remember bath time and lucky for me, I remember the sound of his voice, even after all this time.

—Jenna Cox

The richness of the memories and stories that my friend remembers from her father, even so many years later, are immortalized in her heart and mind. She wishes that she knew more.

Still, it takes courage to share our stories with others. When we share our stories with someone, we are inviting them to bear witness to our full selves, flaws and all, and this is never easy. Our stories do not always present us in the best light. Sometimes we make mistakes, and sometimes we fall down. Sometimes we are the hero, sometimes the villain, sometimes the victim. Our stories are full of tragedy, losses, and disappointments, as well as countless gifts, beauty, and poignant moments. We laugh, we cry, we strive, we rest, we play. We all have experienced plot twists, those unanticipated moments that have changed our paths forever. Tell your story anyway. In our transparency, we become complete. Our past shapes who we are. We need not hate it or be ashamed of it. The lessons we take from the past strengthens us and transforms us from the inside out. Our gift is in our stories.

Telling our whole stories and hearing others' stories help rid us of labels. Uncle Joe is no longer just grumpy, and Aunt Jane is no longer aloof. We are more than smart, successful, lazy, or an addict. We become whole. We can see and acknowledge our efforts and our victories. We can see patterns and tendencies and maybe even see where we need to do work within ourselves. Telling our whole stories means that we are no longer defined by our worst moments. We can see the positive and the negative. We can appreciate that we are multifaceted. There are many parts to us. When we recognize that this is true of us, then we can know it is also true of others. Instead of judging from a photograph, we can appreciate the whole album. The appreciation fosters understanding. Understanding and empathy are the foundations of compassion.

This chapter provides time and space for you to have a conversation with yourself, to ponder who you are, and to tell your story in your own words. In writing your story, you not only create a legacy, but you also have the opportunity to find resolution and a path to creating your own best ending.

Before you begin to articulate your story, here is the first truth to convince yourself of: People *want* to hear your story. Your story is a priceless gift that you, and only you, can share. Your unique story provides a road map for others, especially for your children. But mostly it provides a window into you, and that insight links you to them forever. Your story helps form the connections that we all crave. Your people *want* to know you.

In their book *Living Forward*, Michael Hyatt and Daniel Harkavy write, "We are story driven in the depths of our soul" (Hyatt and Harkavy 2016). With this in mind, take the time to reflect on your own life as if it were a story to be told and passed on. What kinds of things would you include in your story?

To help answer this question, I recently took an informal poll. I asked a large group of people: "If someone dear to you has died, what would you like to know about their life story that you didn't know when they were alive? What do you wish you knew?" Their responses were poignant and provide a template for things you might include in the telling of your story.

■■■ What Survivors Want to Know

1. How would you describe yourself?

2. How does God exhibit himself in your life?

3. What would you want your children to know about you, above all else?

4. How do you want to define your legacy? How do you want to be remembered?

5. What holds value to you? What are your values?

6. What are the most important lessons that you have learned in life?

7. Who has had the greatest influence on who you are?

8. Were you fulfilled? Which of your dreams came true?

9. What do you do well? What are your gifts?

10. What moments of your life were most joyful for you?

11. What were your biggest victories? What are you most proud of?

12. What were your biggest struggles? What worked best for dealing with those struggles and hard times?

13. What would you have done with your life if nothing held you back?

14. What has hindsight taught you?

15. What was your childhood like? Will you share some childhood stories?

16. What did religious practices look like growing up? How did you feel about religion and God as a child?

17. What do you know of your ancestors, and what are some stories regarding your ancestry, grandparents, aunts and uncles, and other stories you could share?

18. What was school like for you? Which subjects did you like / not like? What extracurricular activities were you in? What are some favorite school stories?

19. What was growing up with your siblings like? What was your relationship with them?

20. What is the funniest moment that you recall in your life?

21. What is your favorite way to spend your time?

22. What habits do you have?

23. What sports do you like the most? What sports did you participate in?

24. What foods do you crave? Which foods do you hate?

25. What is on your bucket list? Which items have you accomplished?

26. What famous person do you admire the most? Why?

27. What was your greatest fear? How did you deal with that?

28. What lessons have you learned about love?

29. Describe some traditions from your childhood. What family traditions would you like to see carried forward?

30. What words would you choose to describe your life?

Take some time to work through these questions yourself. Write down your answers in this book or in a safe place, and when you feel ready, use telling your story as an opportunity for some joyful family sharing.

▩■▩ Other Ways to Tell Your Story

There is another way to tell your story that is less of a coherent narrative but can still be meaningful to those who survive you. Often, our personal belongings contain multitudes of stories and meaning to us that can be lost once we pass away. I experienced the power of telling the story of the objects that are left behind after the death of my mother. As I was going through my mother's belongings, occasionally I would find a note on the back of something—a picture or a vase, for example. The note would say, "This belonged to your great-grandmother," or, "I bought this on a trip to …" These small notes gave meaning to these heirlooms that otherwise might have held little value to me.

I know a young lady who asked her father to put a little note inside all of the things that he valued so that she would know the history behind it and why it held meaning to him. She asked him to leave behind a short explanation of the heirlooms she would receive. This would be the greatest gift—the link between his past and her present, the *story* behind the inheritance.

You can gift your children with the stories that connect them to their past. You can include in your legacy descriptions of personal belongings—the story of the things you're passing on. This can be done in a number of ways. For example, you might stick on a brief note using Post-it Notes, and this is an easy way to mark your objects with the personal meaning that they hold for you. You can also itemize lists with a brief description. By sharing the meaning behind your personal belongings, you can add more adventure for the people going through your belongings once you are not here. What could be a tiresome or painful chore becomes a historical treasure hunt filled with delightful discovery.

You could also write personal letters and leave them behind for those you love. I have known people to leave video messages, audio recordings, or years' worth of birthday and holiday cards for their loved ones to have when they are no longer on earth to send them. Imagine what a delight it would be to receive a message from a loved one when you'd least expect it. I can't imagine a more timeless, thoughtful, precious gift.

Journaling is another way to pass on your story. My older sister lived a very troubled and secretive life. Probably in shame, she removed herself from the people who could have loved her. After her death, we found an entire box of journals. They wove a tragic story of addiction, self-loathing, and pain interspersed with joy and self-knowing. It was difficult to read. But, for her children, it filled in the blanks that they always wondered about and helped bring closure. Hopefully, your journals will have much more joy and victories. The truth sets everyone free.

Of course, in this process of telling your story, in whatever way works best for you, do not forget that you are still writing your story every day. Your children, friends, and grandchildren are still looking to you to show them how to live right. You are still modeling to the next generation the things that all of us will one day need to know. You are still teaching, and the rest of us are still learning from you. Please, keep telling us your story.

Chapter 5

Relationships: The Characters in Your Life

Love, when it's hard, is the purest love.
— JOHN TRENT

■■■ Relationships Are Hard

First of all, this relationship stuff is hard work. How could it not be? We are trying to be heard and understood, and get what we want, and get our needs met, and we have so many *differences* to bridge. Every family—indeed, every relationship—has its ups and downs. Many people love each other through the difficulties and come out stronger and closer in the end. Sometimes, however, the chasms can seem uncrossable. We may need help to meet in understanding.

We are completely different beings. Our biology, which makes up our predisposition to personality traits like tolerance and patience, is different. The languages that we use to express ourselves are different; one word can have completely different meanings to people. Our life experiences are different, and with that, we view new experiences through the lens of what we already know. The present is often clouded with our pasts. We have different wants, needs, and priorities, or sometimes the same ones but at different times. Our own life experiences form our own truths, beliefs, and values, and often, variations in these can cause conflict in families.

To demonstrate how each of us has a unique perception of even a single word, I ask my clients to close their eyes. I tell them that I will say a word, and they should draw a picture of the word in their imagination. For example, I say the word *dog* and then ask them to describe what that word brings up for them. I never cease to be amazed by how vast the differences are in interpretation of even a simple noun. Now, imagine we are using more emotionally charged words in a heated conversation, like *honesty* or *trust*, or even super-charged words, like *always* and *never*.

At the same time, I can't tell you how many times I've heard, "Well, he should have said ..." Too many times we tell ourselves what someone *should* have said instead of trying to understand what they were trying to say. We can waste so much time miscommunicating. We pull out the bullhorn when we should be listening, contributing to the exasperation rather than to the healing. Or we turn away and close ourselves off, never having difficult conversations and, instead, accumulating the hurt like a huge heap of trash until it becomes too big to properly dispose of.

If too many of these misunderstandings, miscommunications, and missed opportunities for connection accumulate, our relationships may become broken. When I hear aging people speak of their broken relationships, I often hear a deep need to close the gap and a desire to not leave brokenness. There seems to be an innate call to heal what is broken and to avoid that which sits inside of us as regret. It is hard for peace and regret to live in the same heart.

It is said in common lore, and indeed I believe it, that as we end our lives, no one talks about what we wish we had in terms of materialism. Rather than wealth or prestige, what our hearts and souls long for is peace and relationship. Sometimes, to have that peace, we need to heal, to the extent possible, broken relationships.

We all have broken relationships in our pasts. We all have caused hurt to people we love, and we have been hurt by people we love. We have all disappointed and been disappointed. Sometimes the hurt and disappointment have caused fractures in important relationships. This is not uncommon; it is a truth for many individuals and many families.

Sometimes, oftentimes, the key to healing is understanding and empathy, especially when the brokenness stems from confusion and unanswered questions. These unanswered questions may stem from a basic lack of understanding of another person's story. For example, in my career as a family mediator, I have noticed an interesting phenomenon that often repeats itself in families. This phenomenon is that we often tell ourselves a story about someone else's motives without really understanding what is truly going on for that other person.

As one example, in a family, the stories of the older generation are largely unknown to younger members of the family. Often in the minds of our children, we are born as parents, full grown and powerful. I don't remember ever wondering as a little girl what molded and shaped my parents' viewpoints, many of which seemed in sharp contrast to my own. The other things, so many things that my parents taught me—indeed, hardwired into me—I simply accepted as truth. Their views became my mantras. Often, this later left me confused and alone when I discovered the rest of the world did not necessarily carry the same torch.

I recently talked with Laura, a woman in her fifties who had spent her life terrified by her mother and her mother's constant criticisms and violent outbursts. Laura bears the scars of never feeling good enough—scars that she has carried from childhood through adulthood. When the time came, Laura sat with her mother in her final weeks and did her best to help her mother die peacefully.

However, Laura held a fear within her, even as she sat with her mother. For her entire life, Laura and her sister had heard their mother talk of a book she kept. The mother would say to the girls, "I'm going to put this (wrongdoing) into my book!" To the sisters, the book was a bible of all of their transgressions and all of the anger and disappointment that they had been to their mother. As their mother's end was drawing near, Lisa and her sisters joked nervously. What if this book really did exist? What if they found it after their mother died? Mostly, what if it confirmed to them that their mother really was so disappointed in them?

Laura really did find the book after her mother died. It was not as she expected. In the book, a diary, her mother talked about her own pain and her own struggle with depression, with disappointment, with being overwhelmed, and with feeling incompetent and alone. The book was of a woman struggling emotionally. Laura and her sisters almost felt betrayed. This was not the angry, judgmental mother they had experienced. This new vision of their mother shattered the story they had told themselves and changed the reality that they had known. There was much regret around how relationships might have been different had they known this story sooner. They could have approached their mother with compassion had they known her brokenness and her own struggles with being human.

Unfortunately for Laura's mother and for many of our older generations, feelings were not talked about. There was no one to listen. Work and action were valued, and emotions were taboo. People carried their stories and their pain, raw and unhealed, for their whole lives. Laura and I talked about how the book could still be a gift. Their mother lived in a time when she could not speak her pain. But she wrote her pain.

Writing one's pain, or journaling, is a tool for catharsis and healing that I recommend to many of my clients. Clearly, their mother wanted to be known. She wanted to be seen and understood. She left the book, knowing that someday someone would hear her, so to speak, and maybe her daughters could then know her and understand her and, God willing, maybe even forgive her—a bittersweet gift, indeed.

When we suffer at the hands of our own parents' humanness, foibles, weaknesses, and disappointments, it can be difficult to recognize that they too have suffered from the best efforts of their parents before them. Rather than the omnipotent powers we perceived them to be, they become human—like us. That can be difficult to reconcile—the view of the powerful parent and the weaker child replaced with broken adults trying to raise better children, often without a model in their own lives to show the way. In order to reconcile these conflicting images of people who were hugely impactful to us, it means that we may have to forgive them.

Some of us, maybe many of us, have received the fear and avoidance of emotion from our parents. Others of us may have learned an unwillingness to talk about the difficult things, such as hurt, disappointment, loss, grief, and death. We live in a time now, though, when we recognize that our feelings are too big a part of us to go unexpressed. In fact, it is critically important that we face our feelings head-on, especially as we try to write our stories and finish well. Feelings can be questions that unlock understanding. They are gifts to be shared. When shared, they build intimacy. Though it may be painful, and will certainly not be easy, fully opening ourselves up to the feelings that we may have kept buried deep down is the only way to be able to end our stories with peace and wholeness.

■■■ Fostering Positive Relationships

So, what fosters positive, loving, and connected relationships? Most importantly, relationships require an environment of safety, autonomy, and respect to thrive. We need to create a safe atmosphere, one where there is not too high a price for being honest, especially when honest is hard to hear. This means that if we want to solve problems, if we want people to be honest, we need to be aware of our own words and reactions so that the price someone pays for being honest isn't so high that it becomes too difficult and that person is silenced.

Through my career as a mediator, I have learned that the strongest relationships do the following seven things well:

1. They don't run from fights. The number of conflicts and arguments is often not what says a relationship is troubled, but rather the ability to resolve those conflicts. Resolving conflict strengthens relationships and builds intimacy.

2. They don't hit below the belt. They recognize that words hurt. They are not trying to hurt; they are trying to hear and be heard.

3. They know when to take a break to cool down. It is important when taking a break to agree on a time to return to finish the conversation.

4. They have ground rules for arguments. They agree on what is fair fighting and stay within their agreement. They learn from their mistakes.

5. They acknowledge each other's feelings and points of view. Even though they may not agree, they appreciate the right of the other to have a different perspective and strive to see it from their shoes.

6. They give each other the benefit of the doubt. They try to make positive assumptions about motives at best. At the least, they will ask motives and thoughts and try not to assume them. They remember that, ultimately, they are on the same team. The *us* is at least as important as the *me*.

7. They are committed to having fun and enjoying each other. They celebrate and encourage each other.

In addition, there is a simple guideline that I found useful in my own relationships. It's called the 80/20 rule, and though there are several variations, this is how I learned it and teach it. Think of relationships as a bank. We need to make positive deposits into the bank so that there is value poured into our relationships because sometimes we're going to have to make withdrawals. Positive deposits include gratitude, appreciation, gifts, conversations, acts of service, or whatever is loving and fills the other person. Withdrawals are the tougher conversations. Sometimes it's negative feedback or criticism or stretching the other person with needs. We need to purposefully put in 80 percent positive so that our bank can bear the 20 percent withdrawal. That way, we don't break the bank, and the relationship doesn't suffer.

> With so much to have and hold,
> Under the curving sky, I'm finally
> learning why, It matters for me
> and you, To say it and mean it too,
> For life and its loveliness, And
> all of the ugliness, Good as it's
> been to me, I have no enemies.
> — AVETT BROTHERS,
> "NO HARD FEELINGS"

You may be reading this and worrying that some of your relationships are perhaps too broken to be fixed, but I want to reassure you that it is not too late. No matter what is set in motion, as long as we have breath, there is still time to change our course, to begin to mend broken relationships, and to strive for peace and wholeness in those relationships. Even the most challenging relationship can be an opportunity for forgiveness and healing. I'm not suggesting that you knock on the door of every person you have wronged or you turn the other cheek to someone who has harmed you, but if there is a relationship in your life that is preventing you from being fully at peace—and it is likely that while reading this you can immediately think of such a relationship—then consider beginning to take steps toward healing, whatever that healing looks like for you and the other person. Often, when we can let go of the expectation of what we think the relationship (or the person) should be and accept it how it is, we can begin to have a healthier, happier relationship. Mediation is one tool to help us redefine difficult relationships, and I'll discuss this in detail in the next chapter.

As much as it is important to mend broken relationships, we should also continue to cultivate our happy, healthy relationships with those who are most important to us. Sending love and encouragement to the people we care about doesn't need to end when we die. I think one of the most powerful gifts that we can leave behind could be a personal note to the people in our lives.

As an exercise, take a moment and list the most significant people in your life. How is your life different because you shared time with them? How did they impact you? What are your favorite memories of them? What would you like to say about how you experience them or who they showed up to be in your life? What message do you have for them? Consider sharing your answers with each person in your life or writing them down to leave behind.

Chapter 6

Communication Tools to Resolve Conflict: Beyond Heroes and Villains

Rejection from family cuts deep. Give me
the opportunity and the courage to make
things right with those estranged from me.
— STEVE GRISSOM AND KATHY LEONARD,
*DIVORCE CARE: HOPE, HELP, AND HEALING
DURING AND AFTER YOUR DIVORCE*

As I discussed in the previous chapter, the biggest regrets that we can have, as we write our story, will likely be around hurt relationships. Luckily, we can choose to heal these relationships before it is too late. Just because we tell ourselves it's too late, does not make it so. Remember, it is our story to write. We can come to a place of wanting to resolve conflict when we decide that we no longer want to fight, but that we want to find a way to work things out.

▦ ■ ▦ Conflict as an Opportunity

So, how do we begin to heal relationships, especially when conflict is involved? World-renowned mediator and conflict manager Kenneth Cloke reminds us, "Every conflict is an opportunity for growth and learning and transformation and transcendence" (Cloke 2019). As this suggests, we can move from seeing conflict as a crisis to seeing it as an opportunity. With this new frame of reference, we may find that it is better to choose a solution rather than choosing to be right at all costs. Still, even with the best of intentions, resolving conflict while maintaining relationships is hard.

If we want to resolve conflict, we must first learn how to do so. The field of conflict management can provide us with useful tools to handle conflict. Conflict management includes understanding yourself, listening well, naming the problem, accepting the other person's viewpoint (even if you don't share it), validating the other person's experience as their truth, and coming up with ideas for moving forward. It also requires acknowledging and apologizing for negative, disrespectful, or counterproductive communications; deciding what kind of relationship that you would like to have; choosing an outcome that is completely new and different; and ending with heartfelt acknowledgement and appreciation.

Outwitted
He drew a circle that shut me out —
Heretic, rebel, a thing to flout.
But Love and I had the wit to win:
We drew a circle that took him in!
—EDWIN MARKHAM

Ideally, well before we even encounter conflict, we must first begin by identifying what is going on inside of us. When we are hurt, we often become firm in our positions and hold fast to our truths as a method of self-defense. When we are in this place of steadfast resolution, it can be difficult for us to hear or understand what the other person is saying. When we feel threatened and challenged, we usually begin telling ourselves a negative story about the person and his or her motives. It becomes harder to see the good in the other person. Oftentimes, the same phenomenon is going on with the other person as well, so we become stuck in a cycle of anger, pain, and blame. Too often, rather than breaking this cycle by reaching out to the other person for connection and understanding, we become stuck. And without knowing how to handle the conflict in a way that strengthens our relationship and builds intimacy, we pull away and build distance. Though it can feel scary, reaching out in conflict is an intelligent act and a choice to value the other person and the relationship. To move toward someone in conflict instead of away into our safe corners is a very vulnerable act, but vulnerability is always needed for growth. The effort is worth the results.

The truth is, the most difficult person I ever face in a conflict is not the other person but myself. When triggered, we are, by neurological design, reaction machines. Our tendency to react rather than to respond often adds fuel to an already smoking fire. One of my favorite reminders of this is a quote told to me by William Ury: "Speak when you are angry and you will make the best speech you will ever regret."

At the same time, the most powerful instrument to peace and understanding is yourself. If you can recognize what is going on in your body during conflict and notice when you're getting upset, a mere two-minute break to breathe can help you calm down enough to effectively communicate. During this break, you may consider the following questions: What is it in me that I experience as difficult? Am I feeling shame? Anger? Tension? Blame? What is really behind these feelings? Is this conflict about what is going on right now or a reminder of something in my past?

As human beings, we are each a compilation of stored memories and emotions. Our nervous systems are wired to react to things that feel like threats. It doesn't even have to be a real threat. Our reactions don't take the time to decide what is real and what is not; our brains are just triggered by things that remind us of stored painful memories. This means that very often our deepest reactions have nothing to do with the person standing across from us. Rather, our reactions are usually a response to our past.

Recent advances in the neurobiological study of triggering and conflict have demonstrated this. We are biological, reactionary beings before we are thinking beings. When the brain is reacting, it is not even possible to think clearly. When we can calm ourselves, we can respond more in the way that represents who we want to be and less from a place of hurt and self-preservation. In this process, it is important to name your feelings and then accept those feelings as true. This does not mean that your feelings are wrong or bad, and neither are the feelings of the person with whom you are in conflict. You do not need to change or deny your emotions. Take a moment to notice how you're feeling and acknowledge your feelings without judgment. Maybe then it will be possible for you to accept the other's feelings as also true for his or her story.

In general, being proactive will help reduce the risk of conflict escalating and help you and anyone else involved to identify a solution. Tools that you can start to use to be proactive with addressing conflict, or prevention techniques, include listening well, expressing your needs clearly, speaking in *I*, setting up others to win, asking for what you want, and meeting other people's needs. These are basic principles of conflict mediation, which I discuss in a future chapter, and are the same tools used to handle conflict when it has escalated.

Perhaps unsurprisingly, the most important tool for handling conflict is listening. There is a wise, ancient proverb that says we have two ears and one mouth so we should listen twice as much as we talk. Many people consider listening to be a passive act, but true listening is active and can be hard work. True listening requires that we use not just our ears but also our hearts. Listening deeply in this way may help you answer a couple of questions: Where is the hurt in the other person? What is he or she really trying to say? Everyone wants to be heard, but a greater gift is to not just to hear but to understand.

In addition, I often ask my clients in conflict not only to listen but to listen for what is *right*. We tend to listen for what the other person is saying that is wrong or that we disagree with. This is a normal defense mechanism. We listen for something that we can correct or jump on because we want to win. Instead, we need to listen for what the other person is saying that is right and that we do agree with. We need to find and notice what we have in common instead of focusing on our differences because we can build a bridge this way.

One of my absolutely favorite life lessons came from a friend of mine who is one of the most wise and intelligent people I know. Early in her marriage, she told me, "When I fight with my husband, I am so much better at words than he is that I can always win the argument. Then one day I realized that in order for me to win, I had to make him lose. I want to love him enough that I don't have to make him lose." I sometimes substitute *right* and *wrong* for *win* and *lose*. I want to love someone enough that I don't have to make that person wrong in order for me to be right. This is one of the most powerful guidelines I've known for holding my own behavior in check when in conflict.

This is not to say that we have to agree on everything or that differences are bad. It is true that differences can feel threatening. It is a biological self-protection method to perceive differences, even of opinion, as a possible threat. But are they really? What is lost by being different? Instead of seeing differences as threats, we should acknowledge and accept that our differences make us stronger. They increase our potential. They make us individuals and not clones of each other. Think about how terribly boring the world would be without all of the incredible differences between us!

Instead of fearing and resisting them, we should see and respect our differences. This respect means to appreciate the basic dignity of every human being and to see the humanity of the other human being. In conflict, this respect is to believe that we are all doing the best that we can in any given moment and that all of us fail to bring our best selves forward when we are hurt or triggered. Respect is the most underestimated power we have. When we can sit with and respect the other person just for his or her humanity, we can bring compassion and level the power. We can do this when we listen well.

> The more I mirror their feelings, the more they feel validated.
> —ANONYMOUS HOSPICE CHAPLAIN

At the end of the day, many of us have the same basic desires and needs, especially in conflict. We all just want to be heard and valued and to know that what we say matters. This need to be known and heard and to be loved and understood even when it is difficult—this intimate, loving, painful, fearful story—it's all of our story, really. If we can hold ourselves and others with empathy and compassion, especially in times of conflict when it may be the most difficult to do so, then we can transform our conflicts to something greater—a greater intimacy and understanding. In conflict, there can be fear, distrust, and pain, but there can also be hope and heart. We are born to see ourselves and each other and to grow as a result, and this can be enabled by handling conflict well. We are wired for relationships, not brokenness.

▦■▦ Key Questions for Assessing Conflict

Below are some key questions that mediation uses to help people work through conflict and identify their own roles in a conflict. Next time you are experiencing conflict in a relationship, try stepping away and answering these questions. They can help put the conflict into perspective and refocus your attention.

Questions for Reflection

☐ Whom do you have unresolved issues with?

☐ How do you want to be remembered by this person?

☐ What was the conflict that caused the broken relationship?

☐ What was your responsibility in that conflict?

☐ What is it in you that you experience as difficult?

☐ What would you do differently?

☐ What do you wish the other person would have done differently?

☐ What might it be like to experience what the other person experienced?

☐ What could be done to help you speak or listen more openly?

☐ What do you want that relationship to look like?

☐ How do you want to be remembered by that person?

☐ What is something that you want to talk about that you haven't talked about? If not now, when?

☐ What have you learned about yourself from this conflict/ relationship?

■■■ Apology and Forgiveness

The final steps in the conflict process are exploring apology, forgiveness, and the possibility of reconciliation. As a part of these steps, it is important to learn how to apologize and how to accept apology, as well as how to ask for forgiveness and how to forgive others.

Apologizing is not easy. It's difficult to admit our wrongdoing and our responsibility in a conflict even to ourselves, let alone to the other person. I believe we are so grounded in the shame and blame and pain we received when we were wrong growing up that we just can't admit our mistakes. The price seems too high. We have a terrible fear of what will happen if we confess our mistakes and bad behavior. Will our wrongness be held over our heads? Will we be mocked, laughed at, or punished? Will we no longer be loved or loveable? We take this childhood fear of punishment and move it into adult relationships.

In our adulthood, we tend to define people by their mistakes, making it that much harder to admit our own. We are not just our mistakes. We are the sum total of all of the good things that we have done, as well as our mistakes. If we stop judging ourselves and others by our worst moments, it might be easier to admit our mistakes. We are human. We will hurt and be hurt. We will disappoint and be disappointed. We will make bad choices and say the wrong things. We will mess up. In our relationships, we all need to be safe to make mistakes, to be wrong, and to make amends. Relationships can't last if we don't trust that we will try to heal the connection after we mess up. We have to be able to repair that hurt.

I know this firsthand, and I would like to share a personal story about apology that was a life lesson in choosing pride over relationship. Many years ago I was in an argument with my (then) husband. I had made some decision that he did not like, the details of which I don't remember. It could have been anything—you know, one of those typical, not earth-shattering disputes that is not a big deal until it becomes one because of our defensiveness and reactions. He called me to his office to discuss my mistake. I remember feeling like I was being called to the principal's office back in my school days. We were starting the discussion in a position of him being more powerful, which resulted in me feeling like the bad child.

My best friend called me on the phone at the time, and I explained the disagreement to her. She said, "Kim, just go up to his office, look him in the eye, and say, 'I'm sorry for doing that. It won't happen again.'"

I practically shrieked, "What?!" Why would I do that? I clearly wasn't *wrong*!

She said, "Kim, it doesn't matter if you were right or wrong. Just say it. Tell him you're sorry and move on."

I don't know why I decided to try this. Maybe I was tired of arguing over small stuff. Maybe I wanted a challenge. I went up to his office, and he told me where he thought I had been wrong. I listened without saying a word. Then, I looked him in the eye and said, "I'm sorry for doing that. It will not happen again."

The reaction was unexpected and priceless. His jaw dropped open, and he didn't know what to say. There was silence.

I said, "Is there anything else?"

He stammered a no, still looking surprised and maybe even relieved, but definitely unarmed, and I left the office, walked out into the hallway, and laughed. I had not expected his reaction. He was all puffed up, ready to do battle. The apology transformed what would have been a long and probably fruitless discussion. It wasn't so difficult to do, just to say I'm sorry, and yet, it was.

I'm not saying that is the best way to handle all conflicts. What I'm saying is the real lesson I learned is this: even though that worked to diffuse a situation and restore a relationship, I never began with an apology again. And I know I didn't do it again because of pride. I should have. I've heard so many people talk about apology being a sign of weakness or an admission that the other person has won (which, of course, has to mean that we lost). Standing fast in our rightness and refusing to apologize because we will look weak is not strength. It is weakness. It is too much pride. It is showing up putting rightness over relationship. What really horrible thing can happen if we humble ourselves for the sake of a relationship and apologize for our part? Our heads won't explode. Our arms and legs won't fall off. And though it feels like those things might happen, they won't. What might happen is an opportunity for reconnection.

There are skills to apologizing, just like there are skills for handling conflict. Most of us just haven't learned how to do either of these things well. When we learn them, it can change our lives and the lives of our relationships. My favorite book about apology and how to give a good one is *Why Won't You Apologize* by Harriet Lerner. It is interesting, practical, and fun to read, and I highly recommend it.

In her book, Lerner discusses the wrong ways to apologize. We've all had bad apologies. Some of the worst involve things like, "I'm sorry you feel that way," or "I'm sorry you took it that way." Those are not apologies. Please, please don't ever apologize for how someone else feels! Another bad apology is, "I'm sorry I did this, but you made me do this when you ..." A good apology does not use the word *but* (Lerner 2017).

A good apology takes responsibility for what you did wrong and does not blame the other person. It is heartfelt and sincere. A good apology acknowledges that your words and actions were harmful to someone else (even if that was not your intention) and that you feel remorse. A good apology is not done to end a conversation. (Yep, that's what my apology in the above situation was designed to do, so not a good one.) A good apology is a gift to the person you hurt. You shouldn't do it to feel better about yourself, and you definitely should not give an apology expecting anything back, whether an apology from the other person or forgiveness because you apologized. A good apology comes with no strings attached. You just offer your remorse for your behavior, understanding how your behavior was hurtful (it doesn't matter if that was your intention), and an offer to make amends.

I was on the receiving end of a terrific apology for the first time ever a couple years ago. The person who had inadvertently hurt me said something like, "I am so sorry that I said that to you. I can see how hurtful that sounded. I should not have said that. What can I do to make it right?" I'll never forget the healing power of these words—a sincere apology well said.

> Sorry does not equal trust. Sorry equals forgiveness. Changed behavior equals trust.
> —DR. HENRY CLOUD

After receiving an apology, the person who was wronged can choose to forgive or not. Forgiveness, like conflict and apology, is not always so easy. Sometimes, it takes time to process a painful event and to rebuild trust. There is no perfect formula for forgiveness. There are, however, a lot of wise thoughts about it.

First, we have to be willing to forgive ourselves. For me, that's often a bigger challenge than forgiving others. The disappointment and loss can be hard to let go of. My favorite definition of forgiveness is one that I heard Oprah say: "Forgiveness is letting go of the hope that the past could have been different." It involves accepting that something unacceptable has happened. In his video on forgiveness as part of *The Science of a Meaningful Life* series, Fred Luskin says that forgiveness is "a conscious, deliberate decision to release feelings of resentment or vengeance toward a person or group who has harmed you, regardless of whether they actually deserve your forgiveness" (Luskin 2010). I like that. I don't have to judge whether the other person deserves forgiveness. I can give it because it's who I want to be. And it's what I hope for in my own relationships: my own forgiveness when I have hurt someone.

I read these words in *Daily Gospel Reflection*, University of Notre Dame, by Mike Martin:

> Many of us struggle to forgive those who have wronged or angered us, especially when we cannot avoid future encounters with them because they are a family member, a close friend, or co-worker. There are two approaches that have helped me whenever I struggle to forgive others. First, I try to recall an instance when I did or said something hurtful to a family member or friend and how

much better I felt when we reconciled after that person came to me or I went to them to discuss the situation. I remember feeling grateful for their forgiveness and that we could continue to have a good relationship. Second, I recall the wise words of a parish priest. He said, "Forgiveness is a gift we give ourselves. It frees us from feeling angry and bitter toward others and bottling those feelings inside of us." Both of these approaches give me courage to step beyond my hurt and anger to 'be reconciled with my brother or sister. (Martin 2018)

Forgiveness begins with a choice. It is achieved through knowledge, awareness, remorse, and empathy. It is a process. Forgiveness is not always easy. Depending on the hurt, it can take a long time, if ever, to reach that point. Sometimes, we have to try to forgive over and over again. At times, we move forward with varying degrees of forgiveness. There is also a process of grieving that must be walked before we can forgive. We need to acknowledge the hurt, and then we can choose to move past that. We have all been moved by the transformative power of forgiveness. It has the power to bring healing to a victim, to the perpetrator, and to a relationship. It is to watch something beautiful come from tragedy.

After an apology and forgiveness comes reconciliation. As part of the reconciliation process, we must consider important questions about the relationship at stake. What will our relationship look like moving forward? What would we ultimately like for it to be? How do we right the wrongs? At this stage of the process, we often get stuck in our pain and let a wall come up. Instead, we can choose to have a conversation that decides how to move forward productively. This is a very important conversation, but in order for it to be effective, we need to do this when we are calm, not when we are still in a place of hurt or anger. In this way, we are setting ourselves and the other person up for the most successful conversation possible.

At the end of the day, we should remember that there are always so many other options besides ending a relationship. If we harness the positive memories that we've had together, as well as compassion and understanding, we can build a different relationship, sometimes even stronger than before. The truth is, we cannot be in relationship with anyone without hurting and being hurt and without disappointing and being disappointed. This is entirely normal. This is part of being human.

■■■ An Exercise on Forgiveness

Perhaps this chapter has brought forth emotions or specific cases in your mind that involve a need for forgiveness and reconciliation. If this is the case, take a few moments to think about a specific relationship in your life that could benefit from healing and reconciliation.

You might consider the following questions to prompt you:

☐ How willing are you to see your own responsibility in conflict? How difficult is it to apologize for your part?

☐ What are your own experiences regarding forgiveness? When have you wanted forgiveness?

☐ What does it feel like to forgive, for you?

☐ What does it feel like to be forgiven?

☐ What does it feel like to hold onto anger?

☐ What do you need to forgive yourself for?

☐ What are you holding on to that you would like to let go of?

☐ What would it take to be able to forgive?

You know that phone call you've been wanting to make or that letter you've been feeling compelled to write? What are you waiting for? It's time to give yourself the gift of mending fences, patching up old wrongs, and completely forgiving or asking for forgiveness. This is one of the kindest acts you can ever do for yourself ... and you deserve all the kindness in the world.

Chapter 7

Mediation: Handling the Plot Twists

There is nothing like the death of a moneyed
member of the family to show persons
as they really are, virtuous or conniving,
generous or grasping. Many a family has
been torn apart by a botched-up will.
— JESSE DUKEMINIER AND STANLEY M.
JOHANSON, INTRODUCTION TO 1972 EDITION OF
*FAMILY WEALTH TRANSACTIONS: WILLS, TRUSTS,
FUTURE INTERESTS, AND ESTATE PLANNING*

In a recent article titled "Taxes Aren't the Biggest Threat to Your Inheritance. Family Squabbles Are," a poll of attorneys, trust officers, and accountants agreed that family conflicts are the biggest threat to estate planning (Mercado 2018). Indeed, lack of communication and family drama have been cited repeatedly as the reasons behind family estrangement, long-term bitterness, fractured families, and huge amounts of time and money spent litigating decisions. It makes sense, given how complex families have become. Often, there are families of origin, stepfamilies, adopted families, and those we fall in love with and name into our families. Our ability to connect, be informed, and form our own perceptions around family has increased through the use of technology, convenient travel, and social media. It's just a fact that the more moving parts, the more complicated a system usually becomes. When disputes are underway—and they will be when discussing these tricky end-of-life topics—instead of fighting it out in a courtroom, hiring a professional mediator can help.

A relevant piece in *Forbes* concluded that the best way to decrease these family conflicts around end of life is for older adults to talk openly to their family members about their wishes (Zane 2016). As the number of family disputes over inheritance rises, the solution to these potential problems has been demonstrated over and over as being open and honest conversation about end-of-life issues. As I have already discussed in previous chapters, these are often difficult and emotionally charged conversations to have. Still, I hope I have persuaded you that, though challenging, the conversations can be had, especially with help. That help can be in the form of mediation by a professional mediator. As a trained professional, a mediator can bring invaluable conflict and communication skills at any time during the process of planning for end of life, from early, preemptive discussions to reaching agreements that might be moving toward litigation.

■■■ Why Mediation?

Mediation is a process for dispute resolution and conflict management. It is also an alternative to legal action and a process for resolving conflict that might otherwise be litigated. A mediator is an advocate for both sides who facilitates a conversation between the opposing parties. By facilitating conversation rather than declaring an outcome, mediation allows people to be in charge of their own destinies. In mediation, parties get to choose the outcome that works best for all of the people involved. This ensures better outcomes and better satisfaction with the outcomes. Because of this, mediated outcomes that people come to agreement on tend to not need to be modified in the future. The issues can be resolved and the relationship can be preserved. There is no win/lose. Through conversation and compromise, everyone wins.

Before we launch into the tools of conflict mediation, it may be helpful to first understand where conflict comes from. From my experience, conflict almost always stems from unmet needs and expectations. Our emotions often speak to the state of our needs. When our needs are met, we feel satisfied, peaceful, happy, loved, and calm—the positive emotions. When we feel angry, sad, impatient, and lonely, and especially when we are in conflict, there usually is an unmet need. In this light, resolving a conflict should be straightforward: We simply have to recognize and fulfill whatever need we have that is not being met. And if we could identify what it is exactly that we need, we could ask for it, which would greatly simplify things for all parties involved. Mediation helps us address conflict by helping us identify the unmet needs that are underlying the conflict in the first place. In order to come back to love and compassion, which would be the total resolution of a conflict, we need to find out what is driving the conflict or what is that deeper need.

A basic truth about conflict is that the sooner it is addressed and resolved, the easier it is to deal with. If left unresolved, conflict tends to build and escalate. Too frequently, unresolved conflict can escalate to the point of legal action, which I see as an act of desperation, a last resort. When an issue is so big and so important, we can feel that we have no choice but to become adversaries in court. Unfortunately, there is no way to go to court without becoming enemies. The system is set up for one person to win and another to lose. It makes enemies out of both sides, focusing only on what wrongs are done.

I realize that talking about resolving conflict is easier said than done, especially when people are hurt and the stakes are high. When acting as a mediator or conflict coach, I tell my clients, and it is true, that I am very good at handling conflict— unless it's my own. I've trained in this for many years, and I still can struggle if left to my own devices. Part of the reason for this is because dealing with conflict is a skill few of us have learned. If we think about conflict as a problem to solve, many of us may not yet have the skills we need to do so. It's difficult to listen well, to hear what the other is saying clearly, and to remain calm and open when you are triggered or feeling strong emotions. This is why I think we all may encounter situations where we need a mentor, wise counsel, a professional conflict manager, or a mediator.

A mediator functions as the third person who is advocating for both sides. Our job is to keep the environment safe so that difficult conversations can happen. Through careful facilitation, we help people really hear each other. We guide people in figuring out what the issues are that are underlying the argument by identifying needs and concerns. We help people stick with the fact that the issues are the problem, not the other person. Fisher et al. refer to this as "separating the people from the problem" (Fisher et al. 1999). The mediator's job is not to decide who is right or wrong but to help people find their common ground and find solutions to their problems. If people have the opportunity to tell their stories in a safe environment with caring people witnessing their words, other people often listen. A mediator helps parties involved hear the other side without judgment, express their own needs in a safe environment, build trust through dialogue, and develop a plan for moving forward that is agreeable to everyone.

Mediation, therefore, is not about giving up or giving in. It's about reaching a decision that feels good to everyone. My work as a mediator has shown me that it's never too late, never too difficult, and never impossible to rebuild, redefine, and even restore relationships. Holding a grudge and holding in anger is what is difficult. It is said of bitterness and unforgiveness, "It is like drinking poison and expecting the other person to die." What amazes me every time I work with families is that no matter what the story or how bad things seem, I am *always* dealing with very good people who are acting poorly in their pain. Again, we have just not learned to handle conflict well. And it's not so hard once you learn how. It also helps to have help, which is why I am such a strong advocate of mediation.

There are specific conversations that are conducive to

bringing a mediator to the table to help us have safer, more productive conversations. These include:

1. Estate planning: Having a mediated discussion around estate planning can not only help everyone come into agreement on what decisions are being made, but conversations can also be had to understand *why* certain decision are made. Mediating estate planning helps reduce the possibility of family lawsuits and helps to prevent future problems.

2. Health-care decisions: Still, in our culture it is difficult, if not taboo, to have conversations around death and dying. These are emotional conversations. Mediation is a terrific venue for having open, honest, difficult discussions and helping to become very clear on what your wishes are. It is best to find a mediator with a health-care background for these conversations. She can help explore the many options and provide a clearer picture of what those choices might look like.

3. Contested guardianship / conservatorship action: As mentioned prior, families often do not recover from these arguments surrounding guardianship. They are especially expensive, bitter, and painful processes. Coming into agreement on questions of guardianship helps everyone to have a voice and can help preserve the relationships within families.

4. Funeral decisions: Funerals tend to be an area where people have strong opinions. Coming into agreement before the funeral helps to make sure that everyone has an

opportunity to have their visions honored. It will relieve the stress and differences that might come after our loved one has died, when emotions are already very high.

5. Family dynamics: It is not infrequent that I hold mediations to help families heal. For all of the reasons mentioned throughout this book, at the end of the day, it is our family that is our legacy. Most of us have a desire to heal that which is broken so that we can finish with peace. I like family mediation because it involves not just healing but also making a plan for handling conflict in the future. It is difficult to unpack family problems and rebuild through solutions, yet it is so much less difficult than living with brokenness and bitterness.

These are all difficult conversations. In any hard conversation, we are communicating with our hearts and our heads and our histories. Listening with our hearts can render us with too much emotion and not enough logic. Listening with our heads can leave us with logic but without the feelings that are imperative to recognize the whole picture and find creative solutions. Listening with our histories can leave us stuck in seeing and hearing people through the lens of only our past experiences and perceptions. When emotions run high, as they do when we have skin in the game, when we care, when our futures are on the line, then it is so much more difficult to be open-minded and objective. A mediator can help us come into conflict with fresh eyes and ears. In mediation, everyone has a voice, and each voice matters. We work through the hard stuff and come out not only intact but usually stronger than before.

Conclusion:
Ending with Purpose

> Why do they not teach you that time
> is a finger snap and an eye blink, and
> that you should not allow a moment
> to pass you by without taking joyous,
> ecstatic note of it, not wasting a single
> moment of its swift, breakneck circuit?
> — PAT CONROY

As human beings, we all have needs that, when met, give meaning to our lives. For many, these most basic needs for a meaningful life include to be known by loved ones, to have purpose in what we do, and to leave a lasting legacy. If it is true that these are basic ingredients to a meaningful life, then we should not just leave them to chance. We should deliberately surround ourselves with people to see us and know us, we should pursue actions that align with our sense of a greater purpose, and we should consciously articulate the legacy that we hope to leave behind.

Many people belong to a certain faith and are believers of God and their religion. Most religions celebrate a life after death, implying that life is toilsome, difficult, and painful, while glory, peace, and rewards lay in the afterlife. Indeed, the implication is that the purpose of life is to spend time on this earth and then to die and be with God. In complete paradox to these religious lessons, most of us fear death. We love life because it is all of those things above and so much more. We know that life offers beauty, love, and hope, to name a few.

Erwin McManus reminds us, "Your faith does not make your life easier, your faith makes you stronger" (Global Leadership Network 2018). When we can accept death, talk about it and prepare for it, we will put the fear of death behind us and we can focus on how we want to live. Everyone hopes for a miracle—to be restored to the best version of themselves. In the process of searching for that tiniest hope, sometimes we put people through horrible suffering. I used to know a young man who died in his early twenties of a rare form of cancer. He packed a full, joyful, hardworking, accomplished life in those short twenty years. I will never forget the words at the service from his mother. She said, "I prayed for a miracle. Then I realized *he* was the miracle." Dear people, *your life is the miracle.*

Living forever is not the solution. Neither is living longer. We were born to die. It's part of life. It seems the best way to spend my existence is to be living more fully and purposefully in the moments that I do have. It is to live lovingly, so that if this is a last moment, mine or theirs, that I have as little regret as possible. It is to hold as my guiding light that life is precious. And short. And every moment matters.

Sometimes as I sat beside dying elderly patients, I would be struck by a sense of irony. Here are men and women who worked their whole lives, I would think. Their generation raised my generation, and the gifts they gave the whole world, the lessons and the legacy, are received by me. They sacrificed, loved, hurt, worked, and lived—hopefully fully. Now they are frail, often without a voice and at the mercy of the care and decisions of others. Now they *deserve*. They deserve compassion, tender care, honor, and respect. Of course, we all do, but especially those of the generations before us who no longer have a voice that roars because, without a doubt, they have paid their dues.

I am dying. I am dying, and so are you. No one makes it out of this life alive. Part of being born is that we also, inevitably, must die. This process is natural, like an exhale to an inhale or like night to day. It just is. Despite its inevitability, part of our anxiety about death is due to the fact that we can't know when it will happen. We are afraid of change. We are afraid of what we do not know. But this uncertainty is exactly why every moment matters.

And, again, despite the inevitability of death, we often don't want to look at death or talk about death, except maybe as some horrible robber of our right to life that victimizes us with an unwanted appearance. In this mindset, we are often angry, appalled, and in disbelief when we receive diagnosis of illness, like somehow this is not supposed to happen to us. And even though many of us profess to have faith that we are convinced has a story more wonderful for us after our death, we treat illness and death like a punishment, an insult ... like an enemy.

Time after time, I have spoken with patients and families and clients who are completely shocked and overwhelmed when they find themselves battling illness and even impending death. Faced with their own mortality, so much seems unknown and undone that they don't even know where to begin. Because for most of us, we see illness and death out there happening to other people. We think, somehow, that death and illness will not happen to us.

Last night, I received yet another phone call saying a young person has a rare form of cancer. I wracked my brain. Are there more and more young people getting cancer, or am I at a stage of life when I am more aware of what is going on in other people's lives? What can I possibly say that could make a difference amid so much pain? Yet, as I reflected more, I realized that despite the glaring pain, there is truly a gift in these moments, for all of us, despite the instinct to label this as senseless tragedy. This gift is the reminder that life does not have guarantees. It is the reminder that life is precious and short. Hardship, pain, suffering, and loss—sometimes devastating loss—are all parts of life, but that doesn't mean that life is not beautiful.

Because of these truths, I am reminded that every single moment matters. If I believe that and if I embrace that, then I live with a deeper respect and appreciation of the moments I do have. Knowing that the next diagnosis or the next trauma could be me or someone I love dearly, I have no choice but to be more compassionate and more loving to every single life I touch, regardless of race, gender, religion, or even attitude. How can I do this? I can listen with an open heart, take a moment longer, express appreciation, apologize, and be kind. It could be someone else's last moment. It could be mine.

In this way, beyond writing this book to encourage you to confront your mortality and consider how you want your ending to look and feel, I've also written this book to remind you to consider how you want to live. If we can understand that death is part of our stories and write that part purposefully and have those difficult discussions, then we can create our own endings and embrace our futures. In doing so, we may find great peace and fulfillment because we are honoring our human need to be known, to have our lives be purposeful, and to leave a lasting legacy. As Atul Gawande writes, "You may not control life's circumstances, but getting to be the author of your life means getting to control what you do with them" (Gawande 2014). Hopefully, after reading this book, you feel motivated and prepared to control the circumstances surrounding the final chapter of your story.

Finally, this I know to be true: I have one shot at this journey we call life. I don't know how long I have, but I know that I have one day less than I did yesterday. I also believe that we leave our legacy every moment, every interaction, no matter what we do and no matter where we are from. Every interaction with another person is an opportunity to leave a legacy of kindness or unkindness. Who we are, in any given moment, lives on. We are told in scripture to "number our days." When we do just that by recognizing the finite nature of our days, I believe we can live purposefully, write a beautiful story, and can die without regret.

Afterword: Additional Tools for Your Journey

We all die. The goal isn't to live forever,
the goal is to create something that will.
— CHUCK PALAHNIUK

According to the US census, more than 14 percent of Americans are aged sixty-five and older (US Census Bureau n.d.). The aging population is the most rapidly increasing demographic. AARP found that 41 percent of baby boomers do not have a will (AARP 2012). We are too often leaving the last chapter unfinished. It is time to begin a shift in our society, have these conversations, and teach our children how to have these conversations.

The questions and suggestions in this book are meant to be questions that can be shared and conversations that can be had with your loved ones to create peace and positive memories surrounding the end of life. This book embraces the idea that death is a passing of the torch—an end to our stories and the time for the next generation to write theirs. When we build our futures and write our legacies, we are teaching the next generations how to live better.

It is my hope that the stories in this book and the questions I have asked you to ponder will help you realize the power of your story—the story of your past, your present, and your future. It is my wish that by choosing to look at these difficult topics and have these difficult conversations, you can write your story a little clearer, a little kinder, a little more purposefully, and a little richer. In the end, it is not about how long we live but how well we lived. It's not so much about what we did but who we were. It's not about what we had but who we touched.

There are several additional resources beyond this book that are available for helping people have these difficult conversations. I want to share those with you with the hope that they can provide you with additional guidance and support. These additional resources include, but are not limited to:

☐ AARP Family Caregiving Today: Includes state-by-state advance directives, long-term care calculator, caregiving guides, local resources, free in-person events, online workshops, and on-demand videos.

☐ Aging life care managers: geriatricians, geriatric psychiatrists, neuropsychiatrist, geriatric case managers, and memory care facilities.

☐ The American Bar Association (http://www. americanbar.org) has terrific information on necessary legal documents in the "Trust and Estate Law" section, including detailed information on choosing a power of attorney. Also, they have terrific information about elder abuse, different ways it can happen, and how to safeguard against potential abuse.

- [ ] *Being Mortal*, Atul Gawande

- [ ] The Conversation Project (https://theconversationproject.org) offers guidelines to having conversations about end-of-life health-care decisions. It also includes a free conversation starter kit.

- [ ] Family Caregiver Alliance (https://www.caregiver.org) has forty years of experience offering support, including additional resources for caregivers.

- [ ] Five Wishes (https://fivewishes.org) is an advance care planning program and online support for end-of-life decisions and issues. Newsletters are included. It is a program within Aging with Dignity.

- [ ] Hank Dunn (hankdunn.com) has articles and informed advice on compassionate end-of-life decision-making.

- [ ] Keepingussafe.org: senior driving assessment

- [ ] *The Last Arrow: Save Nothing for the Next Life*, Erwin Raphael McManus

- [ ] *The Marriage Ark*, Margaret Phillips,

☐ Mediate.com (https://www.mediate.com) has plenty of articles about mediation and conflict. Also, the site lists mediators who advertise through them listed by state.

☐ The National Council on Aging (https://www.ncoa.org) gives all kinds of insights on aging issues, including information on living well, care issues, and elder abuse.

☐ National Institute on Aging, Advance Care Planning (https://www.nia.nih.gov/health/caregiving/advance-care-planning)

☐ "Supported Decision-Making Teams: Setting the Wheels in Motion." Suzanne M. Francisco (http://supporteddecisionmaking.org/sites/default/files/Supported-Decision-Making-Teams-Setting-the-Wheels-in-Motion.pdf)

☐ US National Library of Medicine, Advance Directives (https://medlineplus.gov/advancedirectives.html)

☐ "When Do I Want Support," American Civil Liberties Union (https://www.aclu.org/other/when-do-i-want-support)

☐ *Why Won't You Apologize,* Helene Brenner

Best Journal and Diary Apps, according to Techboomers

1. Penzu (www.penzu.com)
2. Day One (www.dayoneapp.com)
3. Diaro (www.diaroapp.com)
4. My Wonderful Days (www.mywonderfulapps.com)
5. Journey (www.2appstudio.com/journey)
6. Momento (www.momentoapp.com)
7. LiveJournal (www.livejournal.com)
8. Evernote (www.evernote.com)

Acknowledgements

Feeling gratitude and not
expressing it is like wrapping a
present and not giving it.
— WILLIAM ARTHUR WARD

No one in their right mind, I am convinced, writes a book. Mine came into existence as a calling, a vision that accidentally fell together in the most unexpected way that only something greater than chance can create. For that, there are so many people for which I am grateful.

Once upon a time, a couple of years ago, I was talking to my dear friend, Jan Smith, about promoting my mediation business. She told me that she would book me with groups to speak about the benefits of mediation, but first, she said I needed to create a booklet that I could pass out to these people. I was horrified. Write a booklet? The task sounded daunting. This booklet turned into the product you now read; my own life story coming full circle with a book that will, hopefully, make other's journey easier. Jan has helped me find answers and resources. She has given me honest feedback and constant encouragement, and no one says, "I told you so," with more love and humor than

Jan. Thank you, Jan and Mike, for being such great friends and family to me.

Shortly after my discussion with Jan, I attended a class led by Dr. John Trent on "How to Write a Book or Presentation." Following the course, Dr. Trent offered to meet with a handful of attendees for a three-month small group. I signed up, and that was the beginning of writing this book. John and his daughter, Kari Trent Stageberg, have walked this journey with me for almost two years. They have generously shared their time, wisdom, knowledge, talents, and connections to people who could help. I am awed by their steadfast and joyful generosity.

Thank you to the people in the world of conflict mediation who helped me bring a better version of communication and of myself to the table. I am deeply grateful to all of these people, especially Ken Cloke, who I consider a mentor, and DeLila Bergan, co-chair of the Association of Conflict Resolution Elder Mediation section. I value your willingness to teach, lead, share, and support, all in the name of promoting peace and understanding. I believe you are world changers, and I am so grateful for what I have learned from you.

I would like to thank my dear friends, Sherry (TD) Welch, Mike Smith, and Lyle Lohmeyer. You all never run out of patience with my incessant questions. Thank you for being tirelessly supportive and encouraging and for believing in me and this project, especially when I have been doubtful. I am honored to call you friends.

I would like to thank my friend and mentor Margaret Phillips. You truly are an angel. You are salt and light to so many. Thank you for the mirror that you hold up to me. I would not be where I am if it weren't for you.

I would like to thank my brother, Steven Rogg; his wife, Phyllis; and their family. We managed to make it through life and through our parents' endings while staying closer than ever. We laugh and cry simultaneously. You are the wisest, kindest, most compassionate people that I know. Your striving to honor the wishes of our parents, no matter how difficult they might be, is the stuff of real, unselfish love. I always say that I want to be like you all when I grow up, and your kitchen table is my happy place.

I would like to thank my children: Tony, Samantha, Jennifer, Ben, Kelsea, Shayan, Caison, Eva, and Trey. You have raised me well. You stretch me, encourage me, call me out, and inspire me to always be a better version of myself. You all are so darned smart, fun, and funny. You have taught me what real love looks like. It is sweet and kind, spiced with difficult. You've also taught me that loving someone where they are is the best kind of love. I am most proud of the fact that we are so very different and still love each other so well.

Special heart to Trey Best. As the baby of the family and the last child remaining at home, I can't imagine what it was like for you, hearing details, thoughts, ideas, and complaints tossed around day after day. So many times, I stole you away for a moment to tweak something on the computer or be the sounding board to my ideas. You endured this with stoicism and encouragement. You would make a great conflict manager.

And back to Kelsea Best. There is no way I could have done this without you. Anyone reading this needs to know that this book would not be what it is without you. I like to think I'm a pretty good writer. Kelsea, you edit it and put your touch on it, and good changes to magical.

I'll never forget John Trent reading the first draft. He said, "This is really good writing, but sometimes, it's just amazing, like this part ..."

I laughed. I told him that I'd written every single word on that page ... except that *amazing* part. "That," I said, "my daughter wrote."

I don't know how much time you put into helping me by editing, encouraging, and letting me bounce ideas off of you. You did that without complaint, while you juggled your own busy, giving life. Thank you is not enough.

Thank you to all of the patients, friends, and clients who have touched my life and graced me with their stories. You have shaped me. For Kelly, Sean, Jacob, and all of the others whose stories ended way too soon, you burned bright and touched many. You are missed every day. Sharing our stories—sharing our lives—that is the greatest gift we can give to one another. I hope that I have told your story well.

Love,
Kim Best

References

AARP. 2015. "End-of-Life Care Conversations for Caregivers."
AARP. December 21, 2015. http://www.aarp.org/caregiving/
life-balance/info-2017/talk-end-of-life-care.html.

AARP. 2012. "Many Boomers Don't Have Wills, Poll Finds."
May 1, 2012. https://blog.aarp.org/bulletin-today/
many-boomers-dont-have-wills-poll-finds.

Brenoff, Ann. 2017. "The System of Court-Appointed Guardians
Continues to Fail he Elderly." *HuffPost Life*. October 10,
2017. https://www.huffpost.com/entry/court-appointed-
guardian-system-failing-elderly_n_59d3f70be4b06226e3f44
d4e.

Brown, Brené. 2017. *Braving the Wilderness: The Quest for True
Belonging and the Courage to Stand Alone*. First edition. New
York: Random House.

Brown, Brené. 2018. *Dare to Lead: Brave Work, Tough Conversations,
Whole Hearts*. New York: Random House.

Cloke, Kenneth. 2019. *The Crossroads of Conflict: A Journey into the
Heart of Dispute Resolution*. Second. Dallas: GoodMedia Press.

Fisher, Roger, William Ury, and Bruce Patton. 1999. *Getting to Yes: Negotiating an Agreement without Giving In*. 2nd ed., reprint. London: Random House Business Books.

Gawande, Atul. 2014. *Being Mortal: Medicine and What Matters in the End*. 1st ed. New York: Metropolitan Books: Henry Holt & Company.

Global Leadership Network. 2011. "Erwin McManus." *Global Leadership Network* (blog). 2011. https://globalleadership.org/quote/leading-yourself/qi201710896/.

Grissom, Steve and Kathy Leonard. 2005. *DivorceCare: Hope, Help, and Healing during and after Your Divorce*. Nashville, Tennessee: Nelson Books.

Hyatt, Michael S. and Daniel Harkavy. 2016. *Living Forward: A Proven Plan to Stop Drifting and Get the Life You Want*. Grand Rapids, Michigan: Baker Books, a division of Baker Publishing Group.

Lerner, Harriet Goldhor. 2017. *Why Won't You Apologize? Healing Big Betrayals and Everyday Hurts*. New York: Touchstone.

Luskin, Fred. 2010. "The Choice to Forgive." *Greater Good*. September 2010. https://greatergood.berkeley.edu/video/item/the_choice_to_forgive.

Martin, Mike. 2018. "Reflection - February 23, 2018." MyNotreDame - FaithND. February 23, 2018. http://faith.nd.edu/s/1210/faith/social.aspx?sid=1210&gid=609&pgid=39534.

Mercado, Darla. 2018. "Taxes Aren't Biggest Threat to Your Inheritance. Family Squabbles Are." *USA Today*. July 21, 2018. https://www.usatoday.com/story/money/personalfinance/2018/07/21/

taxes-arent-biggest-threat-your-inheritance-family-squabbles/799763002/.

Meyer, Elizabeth and Caitlin Moscatello. 2015. *Good Mourning.* First Gallery Books hardcover edition. New York: Gallery Books.

NCOA. 2015. "Elder Abuse Statistics & Facts." NCOA. 2015. https://www.ncoa.org/public-policy-action/elder-justice/elder-abuse-facts/.

NFDA. 2018. "Cremation on the Rise: NFDA Predicts the National Cremation Rate Will Climb by a Third Within 20 Years." National Funeral Directors Association. July 12, 2018. http://www.nfda.org/news/media-center/nfda-news-releases/id/3526/cremation-on-the-rise-nfda-predicts-the-national-cremation-rate-will-climb-by-a-third-within-20-years.

Phillips, Emily. 2015. "Emily Phillip's Obituary on Jacksonville. Com." The Florida-Times Union Obituaries. March 31, 2015. https://www.legacy.com/obituaries/timesunion/obituary.aspx?n=emily-debrayda-phillips&pid=174524066.

US Census Bureau. n.d. "Data." Accessed September 8, 2019. https://www.census.gov/data.html.

Wolfelt, Alan. 2016. "Why Is the Funeral Ritual Important?" *Center for Loss & Life Transition* (blog). 2016. https://www.centerforloss.com/2016/12/funeral-ritual-important/.

Zane, Kerri. 2016. "The Shocking Reason Why Siblings Squabble Over Inheritance and How to Prevent It." Forbes. November 14, 2016. https://www.forbes.com/sites/kerrizane/2016/11/14/the-shocking-reason-why-siblings-squabble-over-inheritance-and-how-to-prevent-it/#3000862864f6.

About the Author

KIMBERLY BEST is a professional conflict mediator focusing on conflict coaching, family mediation, and elder care mediation. She holds a master's degree in conflict management from Lipscomb University. She spent her early career as a registered nurse in intensive care, trauma, and emergency medicine, where she gained valuable experience in the medical system. A mother  and grandmother, she currently lives in Franklin, Tennessee, where she runs her mediation practice.